# Ready, Steady,

# Lunchbox

## cooking for kids and with kids

# Ready, Steady, *Lunchbox*

## cooking for kids and with kids

## Lucy Broadhurst

MURDOCH BOOKS

# contents

# read this first...

Learning to cook can be lots of fun. Whether it's a simple snack or dinner for the family. You might need a grown-up to help you with some of the tricky bits, but don't let them take all the credit!

The real secret to being a good cook is being organised. The first big rule is to read all the way through the recipe to make sure you've got all the ingredients and the right equipment. Don't forget to preheat the oven and prepare any cooking dishes, if necessary. Do any food preparation that can be done first, like peeling, chopping or grating vegetables.

Keep reading the recipe as you go, checking that all the ingredients have been added at the right time. Keep a kitchen timer or clock handy, to keep track of cooking times.

Knowing how to store and transport food safely is very important. You don't want all your hard work in the kitchen to go to waste!

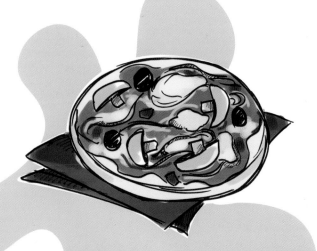

Meat will keep for up to 3 days in the fridge, and up to 6 months in the freezer. To freeze meat, wrap each piece in plastic wrap, then put it in a freezer bag. Make sure you get all the air out of the bag. Label and date the bag. To thaw, put it on a large plate and leave it in the fridge—never thaw meat at room temperature or under water. Do not re-freeze thawed meat unless you cook it first.

Chicken should be treated carefully as it can harbour bacteria. Keep it in the fridge for 2 days at the most, and up to 6 months in the freezer. Thaw chicken in the same way as meat, and cook it within 12 hours of thawing. Never let raw chicken come into contact with other foods in the fridge.

Cool hot food quickly—put it in the fridge as soon as the steam has stopped rising. And always make sure the food is completely cooked through. This is particularly important for chicken and minced meat. When you're reheating food, make sure it's steaming hot. If you are using a microwave, make sure you stir the food while reheating.

If you're packing food in a lunchbox, use one that's insulated or comes with a freezer pack. Don't pack hot foods—first let them cool in the fridge overnight.

## Measuring up

Careful measuring of your ingredients makes for a successful recipe. You will need a set of dry measuring cups, which usually come in a set of four: a 250 ml (9 fl oz/1 cup) measure, 125 ml (4 fl oz/½ cup), 80 ml (2½ fl oz/⅓ cup), and 60 ml (2 fl oz/¼ cup) measure. These are used to measure ingredients such as flour and sugar. You will also need a liquid measuring cup that usually has a lip for pouring and lines on the side that mark liquid measures. Measuring spoons will also be needed to measure small amounts. They are marked and measure 1 tablespoon, 1 teaspoon, ½ teaspoon and ¼ teaspoon.

### Liquid measures

To measure a liquid ingredient, place the liquid measuring cup on the bench, add some of the liquid and bend down so that your eyes are level with the measurement marks. Check to see if you have enough liquid; if necessary pour in a little more. If you have too much liquid pour out the extra.

### Dry measures

Use the correct size measuring cup as stated in the recipe. Spoon the dry ingredients into the measuring cup and level it off with a metal spatula. Cup and spoon measures should always be flat, not heaped.

## Hygiene and safety

1  Always ask an adult for permission before you start to cook. And always ask for help if you are not confident with chopping or handling hot cake tins.

2  Before you start, wash your hands well with soap and water, tie back long hair and wear an apron to protect your clothes.

3  When you're cooking on the stovetop, turn pan handles to the side so there's no danger of knocking them as you walk past. When you're stirring, hold the pan handle firmly.

4  Never use electrical appliances near water. Always have dry hands before you start to use any appliance. Once you've finished using an appliance, switch it off at the powerpoint and remove the plug from the wall before cleaning it.

5  Always use thick, dry oven gloves when you're getting things out of the oven.

6  Remember to turn off the oven, the hotplate or gas ring when you have finished using it.

7  Wash up as you go along. This will save hours of cleaning at the end and will keep your work space clear.

# Before school

# toast toppers

**SERVES 2**

2 slices bread

1/2 tomato, sliced

125 g (41/2 oz/1 cup) grated cheese

1/2 avocado, mashed

1　Top 1 slice of toast with the slices of tomato. Grill (broil) for about 1 minute. Sprinkle with half the grated cheese. Grill until the cheese melts. Slice into fingers.

2　Spread 1 slice of toast with the mashed avocado. Sprinkle with the remaining grated cheese and grill until the cheese melts. Slice into fingers.

**Variations:** Spread toast with mashed baked beans and sprinkle with grated cheese. Grill until the cheese melts.

　Mix together 60 g (21/4 oz/1/2 cup) grated cheese and 1 slice of ham, finely chopped. Spread over a slice of toast and grill until the cheese melts.

**Note:** Toppings can also be put on crumpets and Engish muffins.

# home-made muesli

## MAKES 8 SERVES

150 g (5½ oz/1½ cups) rolled (porridge) oats

2 tablespoons wheatgerm

30 g (1 oz/¼ cup) raw oatmeal

20 g (¾ oz/¼ cup) bran

60 g (2¼ oz/½ cup) sultanas (golden raisins)

30 g (1 oz/⅓ cup) dried apple, chopped

90 g (3¼ oz/½ cup) dried apricots, chopped

1. Combine all the ingredients in a bowl and mix well to combine. Store in an airtight container.

2. To serve, put in a saucepan and pour over a little milk. Stir over medium heat for 30–60 seconds to soften. Alternatively, heat in a microwave for 20 seconds.

3. Serve with other dried fruits, fresh fruit, yoghurt or a drizzle of honey or fruit purée.

**Note:** Some adult commercial cereals can be high in sugar and salt. This muesli (granola) has all the goodness of whole grains and dried fruits without any unwanted extras.

**Storage:** This muesli can be kept in an airtight container for up to 4 weeks.

# healthy fruit mini muffins

### MAKES 16

130 g (4¾ oz/1 cup) chopped mixed dried fruits (such as apricots, apples, peaches)

225 g (8 oz/1½ cups) wholemeal (whole-wheat) self-raising flour

1 teaspoon baking powder

120 g (4 oz/1 cup) oat bran, unprocessed

60 g (2¼ oz/⅓ cup) soft brown sugar

300 ml (10½ fl oz/1¼ cups) skim milk

1 egg

1 tablespoon oil

1 Preheat the oven to 180°C (350°F/Gas 4). Line 16 mini muffin holes with patty cases.

2 Put the dried fruit in a bowl and add 3 tablespoons of boiling water. Soak for 5 minutes.

3 Sift the flour and baking powder into a large bowl, returning the husks to the bowl. Stir in the oat bran and sugar and make a well in the centre.

4 Combine the milk, egg and oil. Add the soaked fruit and milk mixture to the dry ingredients. Fold in gently using a metal spoon until just combined. Divide evenly among the muffin holes.

5 Bake for 20 minutes, or until golden. Allow to cool in the tin for a few minutes, then turn out onto a wire rack. Serve warm or at room temperature.

# multi-grain porridge

**MAKES 16 SERVES**

350 g (12 oz/4 cups) wholegrain rolled (porridge) oats

100 g (3½ oz/1 cup) rice flakes

120 g (4 oz/1 cup) rye flakes

200 g (7 oz/1 cup) millet

2 tablespoons sesame seeds, lightly toasted

2 teaspoons linseeds (flax seeds)

low-fat milk or plain yoghurt, to serve

soft brown sugar, to serve

1  Put the rolled oats, rice flakes, rye flakes, millet, sesame seeds and linseeds in a bowl and stir well. Store in an airtight container until needed.

2  To prepare the porridge for two people, put 125 g (4½ oz/1 cup) of the dry mixture, a pinch of salt and 250 ml (9 fl oz/1 cup) of water in a saucepan. Stir well, then set aside for 10 minutes (this creates a smoother, creamier porridge).

3  Stir again and then add another 250 ml (9 fl oz/1 cup) of water.

4  Bring to the boil over medium heat, stirring occasionally. Reduce the heat to low and simmer the porridge, stirring often, for 12–15 minutes, or until the mixture is soft and creamy.

5  Serve with milk or yoghurt and brown sugar.

# instant breakfast

2 slices fruit bread

butter, to spread

fresh fruit such as kiwi, apple, pear, melon and strawberry

1 Butter the fruit bread and cut into fingers.

2 Slice the fruit into pieces.

3 Arrange on a plate and serve immediately.

**Note:** This is a great start to the day and perfect for fussy eaters who don't like cereal.

# cat french toast

## SERVES 2

1 egg, lightly beaten

2 teaspoons milk

2 thick slices wholemeal (whole-wheat) bread

unsalted butter or oil, for frying

pinch of cinnamon (optional)

dried apricots, raisins and strips of orange zest, to decorate

maple syrup, to serve (optional)

1 Beat the egg with the milk in a bowl.

2 Cut the bread into the shape of a cat face by trimming away the lower corners of the slice to make a rounded chin and cheeks. Shape the top edge into a rounded head with two pointed ears.

3 Dip the bread into the egg mixture, coating both sides.

4 Heat the butter or oil in a non-stick frying pan over medium heat. Cook until golden on both sides. Sprinkle with cinnamon.

5 Add halved dried apricots for eyes, a raisin for the nose and a thin strip of orange zest for the mouth.

**Variation:** You can also use wholegrain, rye or even fruit bread for this recipe.

# junior pikelets

## MAKES 24

125 g (4½ oz/1 cup) self-raising flour

¼ teaspoon bicarbonate of soda (baking soda)

2 tablespoons caster (superfine) sugar

125 ml (4 fl oz/½ cup) milk

1 egg

2 teaspoons oil, plus extra for greasing

jam, to serve

1 Sift the flour and bicarbonate of soda together into a bowl. Stir in the sugar.

2 In a small bowl, combine the milk, egg and oil. Make a well in the centre and whisk in the milk mixture to make a smooth batter.

3 Heat the extra oil in a non-stick frying pan over medium heat. Drop teaspoons of the batter into the pan and cook until bubbles form. Turn and cook the other side of the pikelet (griddle cake) until golden.

4 Serve warm with jam.

**Notes:** These pikelets can be frozen, layered between sheets of baking paper, for up to 1 month.

These carbohydrate-rich pikelets (griddle cakes) are good bite-sized energy food for small children on the go.

# dried fruit compote with yoghurt

### SERVES 4

50 g (1³/4 oz/¹/3 cup) dried apricots, quartered

50 g (1³/4 oz/¹/4 cup) stoned prunes, quartered

50 g (1³/4 oz/²/3 cup) dried pears, chopped

50 g (1³/4 oz/²/3 cup) dried peaches, chopped

185 ml (6 fl oz/³/4 cup) orange juice

1 cinnamon stick

plain yoghurt, to serve

1 Put the fruit, orange juice and cinnamon stick in a saucepan over medium heat and stir to combine.

2 Bring to the boil, then reduce the heat to low, cover, and simmer for 10 minutes, or until the fruit is plump and softened.

3 Discard the cinnamon stick. Serve drizzled with the cooking liquid and a dollop of the plain yoghurt.

**Note:** This fruity breakfast is full of flavour and is a great source of fibre, calcium and potassium with small but important amounts of iron and beta-carotene.

**Storage:** Store in an airtight container in the refrigerator for up to 1 week.

# fruit kebabs with honey yoghurt

### MAKES 4

4 strawberries, hulled

1 banana, chopped

1 kiwi fruit, peeled and chopped

¹/4 small pineapple, peeled and chopped

¹/4 rockmelon (netted melon/canteloupe), seeded and chopped

200 g (7 oz) plain yoghurt

2 tablespoons honey

1 Thread the pieces of fruit onto 4 iceblock (popsicle/ice lolly) sticks.

2 Combine the yoghurt and honey in a bowl. Serve as a dipping sauce for the fruit.

# layered cereal and apple yoghurt

**SERVES 2**

125 g (4¹/₂ oz/¹/₂ cup) low-fat plain or fruit-flavoured yoghurt

¹/₂ red apple, unpeeled, finely grated

70 g (2¹/₂ oz/1 cup) crunchy breakfast cereal

¹/₂ teaspoon soft brown sugar or honey

1  Combine the yoghurt and apple in a small bowl.

2  Layer the cereal and yoghurt mixture in small, wide glasses.

3  Sprinkle the top with brown sugar or honey. Serve immediately.

**Hint:** You can use any type of cereal for this breakfast, such as natural muesli, but choose one that won't go soft too quickly when mixed with the yoghurt.

**Note:** This recipe is a great one for quick starts, as no cooking is needed.

# cinnamon toast

## SERVES 6

120 g (4 oz) caster (superfine) sugar

2 tablespoons ground cinnamon

6 slices bread

softened butter, to spread

1 Mix together the sugar and cinnamon.

2 Put the bread in a toaster. Toast until golden.

3 Butter the toast. Sprinkle evenly with the cinnamon and sugar.

4 Slice the toast and serve immediately.

**Note:** Store the leftover cinnamon sugar in an airtight container to use next time.

# ricotta crumpets with pear

SERVES 1–2

2 crumpets

2 tablespoons ricotta cheese

1 pear, thinly sliced

2 teaspoons honey or maple syrup

1 tablespoon sultanas (golden raisins)

pinch ground cinnamon (optional)

1   Put the crumpets in a toaster. Toast until golden. Spread with the ricotta cheese.

2   Top the crumpets with slices of the pear. Drizzle with the honey. Sprinkle with the sultanas and cinnamon.

**Note:** For added fibre, use wholemeal (whole-wheat) crumpets.

## berry smoothie

SERVES 2

2 bananas, chopped

200 g (7 oz) mixed berries

3 tablespoons low-fat vanilla fromage frais or whipped yoghurt

500 ml (17 fl oz/2 cups) skim milk

1 tablespoon oat bran

1  Put the banana, berries, fromage frais, milk and oat bran in a blender or food processor.

2  Blend or process for 2 minutes, or until thick and creamy.

## breakfast smoothie

SERVES 2

150 g (5¹/₂ oz) fresh low-GI fruit (such as peaches, plums, nectarines, apricots, pears, apples or any type of berry)

60 g (2¹/₄ oz/¹/₄ cup) low-fat vanilla yoghurt

250 ml (9 fl oz/1 cup) low-fat milk (or soy milk)

1 tablespoon malted milk powder

2 teaspoons wheat germ

1  Put the fruit, yoghurt, milk, milk powder and wheat germ in a blender or food processor.

2  Blend or process until well combined.

**Hints:** Experiment with various low-GI fruits to work out your favourite combination for this low-fat smoothie.

## blueberry starter

SERVES 2

200 g (7 oz) blueberries

250 g (9 oz/1 cup) plain yoghurt

250 ml (9 fl oz/1 cup) milk

1 tablespoon wheat germ

1–2 teaspoons honey, to taste

1  Put the blueberries, yoghurt, milk, wheat germ and honey in a blender or food processor.

2  Blend or process until smooth.

## wheaty starter

SERVES 2

2 breakfast wheat biscuits

2 bananas, chopped

60 g (2¹/₄ oz/¹/₄ cup) vanilla soy yoghurt

500 ml (17 fl oz/2 cups) low-fat soy milk

1  Put the wheat biscuits, banana, yoghurt and soy milk in a blender or food processor.

2  Blend or process until smooth.

## summer soy smoothie

### SERVES 4

¹/₂ banana

2 peaches, peeled and chopped

85 g (3 oz) apricot, mango or vanilla soy yoghurt

2 teaspoons wheat germ or oat bran

¹/₂ teaspoon natural vanilla extract

300 ml (10¹/₂ fl oz) plain soy milk or vanilla soy milk

2 teaspoons maple syrup or honey (optional)

1　Put the banana, peaches, yoghurt, wheat germ, vanilla and half the soy milk in a blender or food processor.

2　Blend or process for 30 seconds, or until smooth.

3　Add the remaining soy milk and blend for a further 30 seconds, or until combined. Taste and add the maple syrup, if desired.

## mango juice

### SERVES 2–4

550 g (1 lb 4 oz) fresh mango, peeled

55 g (2 oz/¹/₄ cup) sugar

1　Blend the mango flesh with the sugar and 125 ml (4 fl oz/¹/₂ cup) of water in a blender or food processor.

2　Blend or process on high speed for 1 minute, or until smooth.

3　Dilute with water to serve.

**Hint:** If fresh mangoes aren't in season, use 680 g (1 lb 8 oz) tinned mangoes in syrup and blend to a purée (without adding any sugar or water). Dilute with water to serve.

## yoghurt smoothie

### SERVES 3

250 ml (9 fl oz/1 cup) milk

70 g (2¹/₂ oz/¹/₂ cup) raspberry yoghurt

125 g (4¹/₂ oz/1 cup) frozen raspberries

1　Combine the milk, yoghurt and raspberries in a blender or food processor.

2　Blend or process on high for 1 minute, or until smooth.

## apricot smoothie

### SERVES 2

100 g (3¹/₂ oz) dried apricots

1 tablespoon oat bran

60 g (2¹/₄ oz/¹/₄ cup) apricot yoghurt

600 ml (21 fl oz) milk

1 tablespoon honey

1　Soak the dried apricots in boiling water until they are plump, then drain.

2　Blend the apricots, bran, yoghurt, milk and honey in a blender until smooth.

# little bites

# snack bars

**MAKES 16–20**

60 g (2¼ oz/2 cups) puffed rice cereal

150 g (5½ oz/1½ cups) wholegrain rolled (porridge) oats

30 g (1 oz/¼ cup) sunflower seeds

40 g (1½ oz/¼ cup) sesame seeds

200 g (7 oz) packet dried fruit medley

40 g (1½ oz/⅓ cup) plain (all-purpose) flour

225 g (8 oz/½ cup) honey

45 g (1½ oz/¼ cup) brown sugar

1 Preheat the oven to 180°C (350°F/Gas 4). Line the base and two long sides of a 29 x 19 cm (11½ x 7½ inch) rectangular cake tin with baking paper.

2 Put the puffed rice cereal, oats, sunflower seeds, sesame seeds, dried fruit and flour in a bowl and mix.

3 Put the honey, sugar and 2 tablespoons of water in a small saucepan and heat over medium heat for 1–2 minutes. Stir the syrup into the dry ingredients.

4 Press the mixture firmly into the prepared tin. Use the back of a spoon to spread it evenly. Bake for 20 minutes, or until golden brown. Leave to cool in the tin, then lift out and cut into fingers.

# animal biscuits

**MAKES ABOUT 30**

125 g (4½ oz) unsalted butter, softened

70 g (2½ oz) soft brown sugar

125 g (4½ oz) plain (all-purpose) flour

45 g (1½ oz) rice flour

¼ teaspoon mixed (pumpkin pie) spice

1. Preheat the oven to 160°C (315°F/ Gas 2–3). Line two baking trays with baking paper.

2. Cream the butter and sugar in a bowl using electric beaters until fluffy. Add the sifted flours, spice and a pinch of salt and mix with a knife to a soft dough. Gather together and gently knead for 1 minute. Wrap in plastic wrap and refrigerate for 20 minutes.

3. Divide the mixture into four, then gently knead. Roll a portion onto a lightly floured surface to a thickness of 5 mm (¼ inch).

4. Cut out shapes using biscuit cutters. Re-roll the trimmings and repeat the kneading, rolling and cutting with the left-over portions of dough. Put the shapes on the prepared trays

5. Bake for 10–15 minutes, or until lightly golden. Remove from the oven and leave to cool for 2 minutes, then transfer to a wire rack to cool. Store in an airtight container.

**Note:** If you don't have decorative cutters, you can cut into 5 cm (2 inch) rounds.

# coconut cookies

## MAKES ABOUT 45

125 g (4¹/₂ oz) unsalted butter

230 g (8 oz/1 cup) caster (superfine) sugar

1 egg

1 teaspoon vanilla extract

1 tablespoon white vinegar

65 g (2¹/₄ oz/³/₄ cup) desiccated coconut

185 g (6¹/₂ oz/1¹/₂ cups) self-raising flour

90 g (3¹/₄ oz/1 cup) desiccated coconut, extra

1 Preheat the oven to 180°C (350°F/Gas 4). Lightly grease a baking tray.

2 Beat the butter, sugar, egg and vanilla until smooth. Stir the vinegar into the bowl. Add the coconut. Sift in the flour. Mix well.

3 Roll teaspoonfuls of mixture into balls. Toss each ball in extra coconut.

4 Place 5 cm (2 inches) apart on the baking tray. Bake for 15 minutes, or until golden. Allow to cool on a wire rack.

# munchy oatmeals

## MAKES 28

125 g (4¹/₂ oz/1 cup) plain (all-purpose) flour

140 g (5 oz/²/₃ cup) sugar

100 g (3¹/₂ oz/1 cup) rolled oats

90 g (3¹/₄ oz/1 cup) desiccated coconut

125 g (4¹/₂ oz) unsalted butter

3 tablespoons golden syrup or honey

¹/₂ teaspoon bicarbonate of soda (baking soda)

1 Preheat the oven to 180°C (350°F/Gas 4). Lightly grease two 28 x 32 cm (11¹/₄ x 12¹/₂ inch) baking trays and line with baking paper.

2 Sift the flour and sugar into a large bowl. Add the oats and coconut, and make a well in the centre.

3 Combine the butter and golden syrup in a small saucepan. Stir over low heat until smooth, then remove from the heat. Dissolve the bicarbonate of soda in 1 tablespoon of boiling water and add to the butter mixture, which will foam up instantly. Add to the dry ingredients. Stir until well combined.

4 Roll level tablespoonfuls of mixture into rough balls and place onto the prepared trays, allowing room for spreading. Flatten gently with your fingers.

5 Bake for 20 minutes, or until just golden. Transfer to a wire rack to cool.

# apricot cookies

## MAKES ABOUT 50

160 g (5½ oz) unsalted butter, cubed

185 g (6½ oz/¾ cup) caster (superfine) sugar

2 tablespoons marmalade

1 teaspoon vanilla extract

200 g (7 oz) dried apricots, chopped

125 g (4½ oz/1 cup) self-raising flour

40 g (1½ oz/⅓ cup) plain (all-purpose) flour

### lemon icing (frosting)

250 g (9 oz/2 cups) icing (confectioners') sugar, sifted

2 teaspoons lemon juice

1   Line two baking trays with baking paper. Beat the butter and sugar until creamy. Add the marmalade, vanilla and apricots and mix.

2   Stir in the combined sifted flours. Turn out onto a floured surface and knead until smooth. Divide in half.

3   Place each portion onto a sheet of baking paper and roll up in the paper to form logs 25 cm (10 inches) long. Refrigerate for 15 minutes, or until firm.

4   Preheat the oven to 180°C (350°F/Gas 4). Cut the logs into 1 cm (½ inch) slices. Place on the trays. Bake for 10 minutes, or until golden. Cool on a wire rack.

5   To make the icing, combine the icing sugar, lemon juice and 3 teaspoons of hot water. Put in a piping bag. Pipe stripes over the cookies.

# chocolate banana cake

**SERVES 6–8**

3 ripe bananas, mashed

185 g (6½ oz/¾ cup) caster (superfine) sugar

185 g (6½ oz/1½ cups) self-raising flour

2 eggs, lightly beaten

3 tablespoons light olive oil

3 tablespoons milk

100 g (3½ oz) dark chocolate, roughly chopped

90 g (3¼ oz/¾ cup) walnuts, chopped

1   Preheat the oven to 180°C (350°F/Gas 4). Lightly grease a 10 x 20 cm (4 x 8 inch) loaf (bar) tin and line the base with baking paper.

2   Mix the banana and sugar in a large bowl. Add the sifted flour, eggs, oil and milk. Stir the mixture gently for 30 seconds. Fold in the chocolate and walnuts.

3   Pour the mixture into the tin and bake for 55 minutes, or until lightly browned. Leave to cool in the tin for 5 minutes, then turn out onto a wire rack. Serve with cream, if you like.

## pear muffins

100 g (3½ oz/1 cup) self-raising flour

70 g (2½ oz) soft brown sugar

3 tablespoons milk

2 tablespoons canola oil

1 egg, whisked

2 ripe pears (about 450 g/1 lb), peeled, cored and mashed

1   Preheat the oven to 180°C (350°F/Gas 4). Line 30 mini muffin holes with patty cases.

2   Sift the flour and sugar into a large bowl.

3   In a separate bowl, combine the milk, oil and egg. Add the milk mixture and the pears to the flour mixture. Mix until just combined. Spoon evenly among the muffin holes.

4   Bake for 18–20 minutes, or until lightly golden. Leave in the tin for 5 minutes, then turn out onto a wire rack to cool.

## banana muffins

MAKES 30

100 g (3½ oz/1 cup) self-raising flour

70 g (2½ oz) soft brown sugar

3 tablespoons milk

2 tablespoons canola oil

1 egg, whisked

1 large ripe banana, mashed

1   Preheat the oven to 180°C (350°F/Gas 4). Line 30 mini muffin holes with patty cases.

2   Sift the flour and sugar into a large bowl.

3   In a separate bowl, combine the milk, oil and egg. Add the milk mixture and the banana to the flour mixture. Mix until just combined. Spoon evenly among the muffin holes.

4   Bake for 18–20 minutes, or until lightly golden. Leave in the tin for 5 minutes, then turn out onto a wire rack to cool.

# fruity bran loaf

## MAKES 10–12 SLICES

60 g (2¼ oz/½ cup) chopped dried pears

60 g (2¼ oz/½ cup) chopped dried peaches

125 g (4½ oz/1 cup) dried fruit medley or chopped dried apricots

70 g (2½ oz/1 cup) processed wheat bran cereal

100 g (3½ oz/½ cup) soft brown sugar

375 ml (13 fl oz/1½ cups) reduced-fat milk

185 g (6½ oz/1¼ cups) stoneground self-raising flour

**1 teaspoon mixed (pumpkin pie) spice**

1 Put the pears, peaches, fruit medley, wheat bran cereal, brown sugar and milk in a large bowl. Stir to combine and set aside for 1 hour until the bran has softened.

2 Preheat the oven to 180°C (350°F/ Gas 4). Spray a 9.5 x 19.5 cm (3¾ x 7½ inch) loaf (bar) tin with oil, then line the base with baking paper.

3 Sift the flour and mixed spice into a bowl, then return any husks to the bowl. Stir into the fruit mixture. Spoon the mixture into the prepared tin and smooth the surface.

4 Bake for 45–50 minutes, or until lightly browned. Leave in the tin for 10 minutes, then turn out onto a wire rack to cool completely.

**Note:** This loaf will keep refrigerated for up to 1 week and frozen for up to 1 month.

# muesli and fruit mix

SERVES 5

50 g (1³/₄ oz/¹/₂ cup) plain or assorted rice crackers

50 g (1³/₄ oz/¹/₂ cup) banana crisps

30 g (1 oz/¹/₂ cup) shredded or flaked coconut

60 g (2¹/₄ oz/¹/₂ cup) sultanas (golden raisins)

60 g (2¹/₄ oz/¹/₂ cup) raisins

100 g (3¹/₂ oz/1 cup) toasted muesli

100 g (3¹/₂ oz/2 cups) popcorn

60 g (2¹/₄ oz/¹/₂ cup) sunflower kernels or pepitas (pumpkin seeds)

1   Combine all the ingredients in a large bowl.

2   Spoon into an airtight container. Serve in small containers or individual zip-lock bags.

# bits and pieces with dip

## SERVES 4

### tzatziki

2 Lebanese (short) cucumbers, deseeded and grated

185 g (6$^1$/$_2$ oz/$^3$/$_4$ cup) plain yoghurt

2 garlic cloves, crushed

1 teaspoon lemon juice

1 teaspoon chopped dill

$^1$/$_4$ teaspoon chopped mint

### hummus

220 g (7$^3$/$_4$ oz/1 cup) dried chickpeas

4 tablespoons olive oil, plus extra to drizzle

3–4 tablespoons lemon juice

2 garlic cloves, crushed

2 tablespoons tahini

1 tablespoon ground cumin

### avocado dip

$^1$/$_2$ avocado

30 g (1 oz/$^1$/$_4$ cup) grated cheddar cheese

$^1$/$_4$ tomato, chopped

cottage cheese, to serve (optional)

selection of sliced blanched vegetables (see Hint), to serve

small pieces of cheese, to serve

1 To make the tzatziki, mix the cucumber with the remaining ingredients and serve with the sliced vegetables. If you like, offer some poppadoms or chunks of bread.

2 To make the hummus, soak the chickpeas in water for 8 hours, or overnight. Drain. Put in a saucepan and cover with cold water. Bring to the boil and cook for 50–60 minutes. Drain, keeping 250 ml (9 fl oz/1 cup) of the cooking liquid. Put the chickpeas in a food processor with the oil, lemon juice, garlic, tahini and cumin. Blend well until the mixture starts to look thick and creamy. With the motor running, gradually add the cooking liquid until the mixture is as thick or thin as you like it. Transfer to a bowl and drizzle with olive oil.

3 To make the avocado dip, combine the avocado, cheese and tomato.

4 Arrange small pieces of cheese and vegetable sticks in a lunchbox or small container. Serve with the dips.

**Hint:** Choose your favourite vegetables or a selection which might include cauliflower, baby corn, broccoli, spring onion (scallion), beans, snow peas (mangetout), mushrooms, celery, zucchini (courgette), cucumber, capsicum (pepper), carrot and cherry tomatoes.

# carrot and zucchini muffins

MAKES 18

35 g (1¼ oz/¼ cup) wholemeal flour

30 g (1 oz/¼ cup) plain (all-purpose) flour

1 teaspoon baking powder

1 tablespoon soft brown sugar

½ small carrot, grated

¼ small zucchini (courgette), grated

½ tablespoon poppy seeds

30 g (1 oz) unsalted butter, melted

1 egg white, lightly beaten

2 tablespoons milk

1 Preheat the oven to 210°C (415°F/Gas 6–7). Line 18 mini muffin holes with patty cases.

2 Sift the flours and baking powder in a bowl. Add the brown sugar, carrot, zucchini and poppy seeds. Mix.

3 Combine the butter, egg white and milk. Add the milk mixture to the dry ingredients. Using a wooden spoon, stir until ingredients are just combined.

4 Divide the mixture evenly among the muffin holes. Bake for 20 minutes, or until golden.

5 Cool for 5 minutes, then turn out onto a wire rack to cool.

# spinach and feta muffins

MAKES 20

90 g (3¼ oz) English spinach leaves

155 g (5½ oz) self-raising flour

¼ teaspoon paprika

60 g (2¼ oz) feta cheese, crumbled

2 spring onions (scallions), finely chopped

¼ tablespoon chopped fresh dill

125 ml (4 fl oz/½ cup) buttermilk

1 egg, lightly beaten

2 tablespoons olive oil

30 g (1 oz) feta cheese, crumbled, extra

1 Preheat the oven to 200°C (400°F/Gas 6). Lightly grease 20 mini muffin holes.

2 Steam the spinach until just tender. Drain and squeeze out any excess liquid. Chop finely.

3 Sift the flour and paprika into a bowl and stir in the feta, spring onion and dill. Make a well in the centre.

4 Combine the buttermilk, half the beaten egg mixture and the oil. Add the spinach and fold gently.

5 Divide the mixture evenly among the muffin holes. Sprinkle the feta over the top. Bake for 25 minutes, or until golden. Cool for 5 minutes, then turn out onto a wire rack to cool.

# tomato, bocconcini and basil muffins

**MAKES 24**

170 g (6 oz) self-raising flour

1/2 teaspoon baking powder

185 ml (6 fl oz/3/4 cup) milk

1 egg, beaten

1 roma (plum) tomato, chopped

2 bocconcini (fresh baby mozzarella cheese), chopped

1 1/2 tablespoons shredded basil

30 g (1 oz) unsalted butter, melted and cooled

1 Preheat the oven to 200°C (400°F/Gas 6). Lightly grease 24 mini muffin holes.

2 Sift the flour and baking powder into a large bowl. Make a well in the centre.

3 Whisk the milk and eggs together, then pour into the well. Add the tomato, bocconcini, basil and melted butter. Fold gently until just combined—the mixture should be lumpy.

4 Divide the mixture evenly among the muffin holes. Bake for 25 minutes, or until golden. Cool for 5 minutes, then turn out onto a wire rack.

# parmesan, pumpkin and zucchini muffins

100 g (3$^1$/$_2$ oz) pumpkin (winter squash), peeled and roughly chopped

125 g (4$^1$/$_2$ oz/1 cup) self-raising flour

$^1$/$_4$ teaspoon baking powder

35 g (1$^1$/$_4$ oz) grated parmesan cheese

$^1$/$_2$ zucchini (courgette), grated

60 g (2$^1$/$_4$ oz) unsalted butter, melted and cooled

1 egg

100 ml (3$^1$/$_2$ oz) milk

$^1$/$_2$ tablespoon sesame seeds

2 tablespoons grated parmesan cheese, extra

1  Preheat the oven to 190°C (375°F/ Gas 5). Line 30 mini muffin holes with paper cases. Steam the pumpkin for 10 minutes. Mash until smooth.

2  Sift the flour and baking powder into a bowl, then mix in the parmesan. Make a well in the centre.

3  Put the pumpkin, zucchini and butter in a separate bowl. Beat the egg. Combine half of the beaten egg and the milk and add to the pumpkin mixture. Mix.

4  Add to the dry ingredients. Fold in gently.

5  Divide the mixture evenly among the muffin holes. Sprinkle with the sesame seeds and extra parmesan.

6  Bake for 35 minutes, or until golden. Cool for 5 minutes, then turn out onto a wire rack.

# small finger sandwiches

**MAKES 2**

6 slices bread

**fillings**

50 g (1¾ oz) sliced smoked chicken

½ avocado, mashed

1  Top 2 slices of bread with a slice of chicken breast and then top each with another slice of bread.

2  Spread a thin layer of the avocado mixture over each slice of bread. Top with the remaining 2 slices of bread. Press sandwiches firmly together. Set aside. Refrigerate for at least an hour.

3  Cut the crust from the sandwiches. Cut into a variety of shapes and sizes using decorative biscuit cutters.

**Variations:** You can make these sandwiches with other combinations, such as cream cheese and sundried tomatoes.

You can also replace the sliced chicken with leg ham or slices of turkey breast. Or use sliced cheese instead of meat.

# mini quiche lorraines

**MAKES 12**

2 sheets frozen ready-rolled shortcrust (pie) pastry, thawed

1 tomato, chopped

60 g (2¼ oz/½ cup) grated cheddar cheese

40 g (1½ oz/¼ cup) chopped ham or bacon

1 spring onion (scallion), finely chopped

125 ml (4 fl oz/½ cup) milk

1 egg

1   Preheat the oven to 200°C (400°F/Gas 6).

2   Cut the pastry into 12 circles with an 8 cm (3¼ inch) cutter. Line 12 shallow patty pans or mini muffin tins with the pastry.

3   Mix together the tomato, cheese, ham and spring onion and spoon the mixture into the pastry cases.

4   Whisk together the milk and egg. Pour enough into each pastry case to cover the filling.

5   Bake for 15–20 minutes, or until the filling is set and golden. Transfer to a wire rack to cool. Store in the refrigerator in an airtight container for up to two days.

**Variations:** There are many different combinations of ingredients you can use. Try semi-dried (sun-blushed) tomatoes, feta and thyme; chopped black olives, ricotta and chicken; and tinned salmon, capers and cream cheese.

# cheese pinwheels

### MAKES ABOUT 12

125 g (4½ oz/1 cup) grated cheddar cheese

60 g (2¼ oz) feta cheese, crumbled

1 tablespoon ricotta cheese

15 g (½ oz) chopped spring onions
(scallions)

½ small tomato, chopped

1 egg, beaten

2 sheets ready-rolled puff pastry

milk, to brush

1 Preheat the oven to 220°C (425°F/Gas 7). Line a baking tray with baking paper.

2 Combine the cheeses, spring onion, tomato and two-thirds of the egg in a bowl.

3 Divide the cheese mixture into two and spread over 2 sheets of puff pastry, leaving a 1 cm (½ inch) border.

4 Roll up and trim the ends. Cut into 1.5 cm (5/8 inch) wheels and place on the baking tray. Brush with the leftover egg.

5 Bake for 12–15 minutes, or until puffed and golden. Cool for 5 minutes, then put on a wire rack to cool. Store in an airtight container.

# sun-dried tomato plaits

### MAKES 8

1 sheet frozen puff pastry, thawed

1 egg, beaten

40 g (1½ oz) semi-dried (sun-blushed)
tomatoes, sliced

1 Preheat the oven to 210°C (415°F/Gas 6–7). Lightly grease a baking tray.

2 Lightly brush the puff pastry with the egg. Cut into 1 cm (½ inch) strips.

3 Join three strips together at the top, by pressing. Plait them together, putting slices of semi-dried tomato in the plait.

4 Place the plaits on the baking tray and bake for 10–15 minutes, or until puffed and golden. Cool for 5 minutes, then put on a wire rack to cool. Store in an airtight container.

# chickpea fritters

MAKES 6

2 tablespoons canola oil

4 spring onions (scallions), sliced

2 garlic cloves, chopped

600 g (1 lb 5 oz) tinned chickpeas, rinsed and drained

1 egg

small cos (romaine) lettuce leaves, to serve

crusty bread, to serve

1 Heat 2 teaspoons of the oil in a large non-stick frying pan over medium heat. Add the spring onions and garlic and cook, stirring, for 1–2 minutes, or until the spring onion softens.

2 Put the chickpeas and spring onion mixture in a food processor. Process for about 2 minutes. Transfer to a bowl and mix in the egg. Using your hands, shape the mixture into six fritters.

3 Heat the remaining oil in a large non-stick frying pan over medium heat. Add the chickpea fritters and cook for 2 minutes on each side, or until golden. Drain on paper towels. Serve with lettuce and crusty bread.

**Note:** These fritters are an excellent source of fibre and provide good amounts of protein and iron too.

# corn and capsicum fritters

### SERVES 4

4 tablespoons oil

300 g (10$\frac{1}{2}$ oz/1$\frac{1}{2}$ cups) tinned corn kernels, drained

1 large red capsicum (pepper), chopped

2 tablespoons chopped flat-leaf (Italian) parsley

3 eggs, beaten

sour cream, to serve

1 Heat 2 tablespoons of oil in a frying pan over medium heat. Add the corn and cook, stirring, for 2 minutes. Add the capsicum and stir for another 2 minutes. Put in a bowl. Add the parsley and mix.

2 Stir the beaten egg into the vegetable mixture.

3 Heat another 2 tablespoons of oil in a non-stick frying pan over medium heat. Drop large tablespoons of the mixture into the pan. Cook for 1–2 minutes, or until golden brown. Turn and cook the other side.

4 Drain on paper towels. Serve with sour cream and a green salad.

# potato and leek fritters

### MAKES 40

600 g (1 lb 5 oz) all-purpose potatoes, peeled and grated

1 leek, finely chopped

2 eggs, lightly beaten

1 tablespoon rice flour

2 tablespoons canola oil

1 Put the potato and leek in a bowl. Add the eggs and rice flour and mix.

2 Heat the oil in a large non-stick frying pan. Drop tablespoons of the mixture into the pan. Cook for 1–2 minutes, or until golden brown. Turn and cook the other side.

3 Drain on paper towels. Serve cold either on their own or with baked beans.

# vegetable frittata squares with hummus

## MAKES 30 PIECES

1 large red capsicum (pepper)

250 g (9 oz) orange sweet potato, cut into 1 cm (1/2 inch) slices

1 1/2 tablespoons olive oil

1 leek, finely sliced

125 g (4 1/2 oz) zucchini (courgettes), thinly sliced

300 g (10 1/2 oz) eggplant (aubergines), cut into 1 cm (1/2 inch) slices

4 eggs, lightly beaten

1 tablespoon finely chopped basil

60 g (2 1/4 oz) grated parmesan cheese

100 g (3 1/2 oz) ready-made hummus

1  Cut the capsicum into large pieces, removing the seeds and membrane. Place, skin side up, under a hot grill (broiler) until the skin blackens and blisters. Cool in a plastic bag. Peel.

2  Cook the sweet potato in a saucepan of boiling water for 4–5 minutes, or until just tender. Drain.

3  Heat 1 tablespoon of the oil in a frying pan. Add the leek and stir over medium heat for 1 minute, or until soft. Add the zucchini and cook for 2 minutes, then remove from the pan.

4  Heat the leftover oil. Cook the eggplant for 2 minutes each side, or until golden. Line the base of the pan with half the eggplant, then the leek and zucchini. Top with the capsicum, left-over eggplant and sweet potato.

5  Combine the eggs, basil, and parmesan. Pour the mixture over the vegetables. Cook over low heat for 15 minutes. Put the pan under a hot grill (broiler) until golden. Cool, then flip onto a chopping board. Cut into 30 squares. Top with hummus.

# rice paper rolls

**MAKES 10 (SERVES 2–4)**

½ small carrot

½ Lebanese (short) cucumber

60 g (2¼ oz) finely shredded red cabbage

2 spring onions (scallions)

1 small handful mint, torn

1 small handful coriander (cilantro) leaves

10 x 16 cm (8 x 6 inch) rice paper wrappers

sweet chilli sauce, or soy sauce, for dipping

1 Cut the carrot into 4 cm (1½ inch) lengths. Cut the cucumber into 4 cm (1½ inch) lengths. Thinly slice the spring onions on the diagonal.

2 Put the cabbage, carrot, cucumber, spring onions, mint and coriander in a large bowl and toss.

3 Working with one wrapper at a time, dip into a bowl of hot water for 10 seconds, or until softened. Drain, then lay out on a flat surface.

4 Put 2–3 tablespoons of the mixture on one side of the wrapper, leaving a border at the sides.

5 Fold in the sides and roll up tightly. Cover with a damp cloth and repeat with the remaining filling and wrappers to make 10 rolls. Serve with sauce for dipping.

# vegetable pouches

**MAKES 16–20**

130 g (4³/₄ oz/1 cup) buckwheat flour

2 eggs

315 ml (10³/₄ fl oz/1¹/₄ cups) water

canola oil, for greasing

**vegetable filling**

1 tablespoon canola oil

2 garlic cloves, crushed

75 g (2¹/₂ oz/1 cup) shredded red cabbage

140 g (5 oz/1 cup) finely chopped celery

155 g (5¹/₂ oz/1 cup) peas, cooked

4 spring onions (scallions), chopped

16–20 chives, softened in hot water

cottage cheese, for dipping

1 Sift the flour into a bowl and make a well in the centre. Add the combined egg and water. Beat until well combined and smooth.

2 Heat the oil in a large frying pan over medium heat. Pour in just enough batter to make a thin layer over the bottom of the pan. When the top of the pancake starts to set, turn it over. After browning the second side, transfer to a plate and keep warm. Repeat with the remaining batter.

3 To make the vegetable filling, heat the oil in a frying pan over medium heat. Add the garlic and cook for 1 minute. Add the cabbage, celery, peas and spring onions. Cook for 3–4 minutes.

4 Spoon the vegetable filling into the centre of each pancake.

5 Bring up the edges of the pancake to form a pouch. Serve with cottage cheese for dipping.

# chickpea and parsley salad

## SERVES 2

220 g (7¾ oz) tinned chickpeas

1 large tomato

1 tablespoon chopped flat-leaf (Italian) parsley

1 teaspoon chopped mint

1 tablespoon lemon juice

1½ tablespoon plain yoghurt

1　Drain the chickpeas, rinse under cold running water and drain again.

2　Chop the tomato into 1 cm (½ inch) pieces. Put in a bowl with the drained chickpeas, parsley and mint.

3　Combine the lemon juice and yoghurt in a small bowl. Pour over the chickpeas and mix.

**Note:** Chickpeas make a perfect meal, as they are a great source of vegetable protein, many vitamins and minerals, especially iron.

# nibbler's salad

**SERVES 1**

½ small celery stick

½ small carrot

2 small pieces low-fat cheddar cheese

2 small cherry tomatoes

2 strawberries

1 slice tinned pineapple

2 tinned apricot halves

1 Cut celery, carrot and cheese into sticks.

2 Cut the tomatoes and strawberries in half. Cut the pineapple into pieces.

3 Combine all the ingredients in an airtight container.

**Note:** You can substitute any seasonal fruits for the above suggestions. Try using apples, bananas, pears or peaches. Avoid fruits with seeds, though, unless you can remove them first.

# fruity cheese salad

## SERVES 1

3 dried apricot halves

1 dried pear half

4 dried apple rings

3 dried prunes

4 tablespoons apple juice

90 g (3¼ oz/⅓ cup) low-fat cottage cheese

2 rice cakes

1   Combine the apricots, pear, apple and prunes in a small saucepan with the apple juice.

2   Bring to the boil over medium heat. Cook for 5 minutes, or until all the liquid is absorbed. Allow to cool completely.

3   Arrange the cooled fruit in an airtight container with the cottage cheese. Wrap rice cakes separately to keep fresh.

# fresh fruit salad

## SERVES 2-3

100 g (3½ oz) seedless watermelon, cut into 2 cm (¾ inch) cubes

100 g (3½ oz) rockmelon, cut into 2 cm (¾ inch) cubes

60 g (2¼ oz) strawberries, hulled and cut into quarters

½ kiwi fruit, peeled and cut into pieces

50 g (1¾ oz) seedless white grapes, halved

¼ banana, sliced

1–2 tablespoons unsweetened fruit juice or orange juice

1 Place the fruits in a lunchbox or small container, pour over the orange juice and toss.

2 Serve as finger food or cut up into smaller pieces.

**Note:** You can substitute any seasonal fruits for the above suggestions. Try using apples, pears or peaches. Avoid fruits with seeds, though, unless you can remove them first.

big bites

# sandwich fillings

It can be hard thinking up new sandwich fillings each day. Try some of these yummy combos.

## fillings

- Lettuce, grated carrot, cucumber, beetroot, tomato and cottage cheese
- Egg and tomato
- Vegemite, low-fat cheddar cheese, cucumber and lettuce
- Peanut butter and banana (see note)
- Chicken, lettuce and low-fat mayonnaise
- Ham, low-fat cheddar cheese and cos (romaine) lettuce
- Hummus and bean sprouts
- Ham or chicken, low-fat cheddar cheese and tomato
- Cottage cheese, grated carrot and avocado
- Banana, mashed, with honey and lemon juice
- Lean roast beef, grated zucchini and tomato slices
- Grated carrot, grated zucchini, beetroot and low-fat cheddar cheese
- Grated zucchini, carrot and cottage cheese
- Chicken, low-fat natural yoghurt and lettuce or sprouts
- Banana, low-fat cottage cheese and honey
- Ham, cream cheese and tomato slices

**Notes:** Use a variety of breads (such as wholemeal, wholegrain, rye, pita, rolls, bagels, sourdough, lavash or Turkish) for making sandwiches.

Serve with milk or diluted fruit juice for a quick nutritious lunch.

Some schools may not permit the use of peanut butter in school lunches due to nut allergies. Check before packing sandwiches made with peanut butter.

# gluten-free bread rolls

## MAKES 8 INDIVIDUAL LOAVES

canola oil, for greasing

15 g (1/2 oz) dried yeast (4 teaspoons)

1 tablespoon soft brown sugar

500 ml (17 fl oz/2 cups) warm water

2 teaspoons guar gum (from health food stores)

300 g (10½ oz/2 cups) soy-free, gluten-free plain (all-purpose) flour

130 g (4¾ oz/¾ cup) rice flour

2 teaspoons ground sea salt

45 g (1½ oz/½ cup) rice bran

60 g (2¼ oz) dairy-free margarine, melted and cooled

canola oil, for brushing

1 Preheat the oven to 200°C (400°F/Gas 6). Lightly grease eight 10 x 5.5 x 3.5 cm (4 x 2¼ x 1½ inch) individual loaf (bar) tins.

2 Combine the yeast, sugar and warm water in a bowl. Stand the bowl in a warm place for about 10 minutes, or until the mixture is frothy.

3 Sift the gum and flours into a large bowl. Add the salt and rice bran. Make a well in the centre and add the yeast mixture and cooled margarine.

4 Mix well to form a soft dough. Divide into eight portions, then shape each into an oval shape. Put in the prepared tins.

5 Cover and leave in a warm place for 45 minutes, or until the mixture comes to the top of the tins.

6 Bake for 25–30 minutes, or until cooked through. Remove from the tins and leave to cool on a wire rack.

3

4

# cheese tabouleh wraps

2 pieces lavash bread or other flatbread

2 tablespoons low-fat mayonnaise

8 slices low-fat cheddar cheese

**Tabouleh**

90 g (3¹/₄ oz) couscous

2 tablespoons olive oil

6 tablespoons reduced-salt chicken stock

2 tablespoons chopped flat-leaf (Italian) parsley

1 small tomato, finely chopped

2 tablespoons lemon juice

1. Spread the bread with mayonnaise and top each with two slices of cheese.

2. Put the couscous in a bowl, add ¹/₂ teaspoon of the oil and rub the oil into the couscous grains with your fingers to coat evenly.

3. Put the stock in a saucepan and bring to the boil. Add the stock to the couscous, cover and set aside for 5 minutes. Fluff up the grains with a fork and add the parsley, tomato, remaining olive oil and lemon juice to taste.

4. Spread the couscous over the top of the cheese, leaving a 2 cm (³/₄ inch) gap at one short end. Roll up to enclose the filling. Cut in half to serve.

# falafel rollups

## MAKES 4

4 spring onions (scallions), chopped

15 g (½ oz) roughly chopped flat-leaf (Italian) parsley

1 handful coriander (cilantro) leaves

1 teaspoon ground coriander

1 teaspoon ground cumin

pinch of chilli powder

1 garlic clove, crushed

150 g (5½ oz) tinned chickpeas, rinsed and drained

plain (all-purpose) flour, to coat

oil, for cooking

2 tablespoons ready-made hummus

2 rounds Lebanese bread, cut in half

100 g (3½ oz) ready-made tabouleh (see page 81)

1 Put the spring onion, parsley and coriander in a food processor, and process until finely chopped.

2 Add the spices, garlic and chickpeas, and process to a smooth paste.

3 Shape into 12 patties. Coat lightly in flour and refrigerate for 45 minutes.

4 Fill a deep heavy-based saucepan one-third full of oil and heat to 180°C (350°F), or until a bread cube browns in 15 seconds.

5 Cook the falafel in batches for 2–3 minutes, or until browned and cooked through. Drain on paper towels.

6 To serve, split the Lebanese bread halves. Spread the hummus over the bread, top with the tabouleh and three falafel each. Roll up and wrap in baking paper.

# ham, cheese, tomato and rocket sandwich

**SERVES 1**

2 thick slices bread

1 slice tasty cheese

1 small handful rocket (arugula) leaves

mixed salad leaves

1 small tomato, sliced

2 slices ham

1 Top 1 slice of bread with the cheese, rocket, salad leaves, tomato and ham.

2 Garnish with sliced gherkin (pickle), if desired. Top with a slice of bread.

# wholegrain tuna mayo sandwiches

MAKES 2

100 g (3¹/₂ oz) tinned tuna in spring water, drained

¹/₂ carrot, grated

1 spring onion (scallion), finely chopped

45 g (1¹/₂ oz) low-fat mayonnaise

6 coral lettuce leaves, washed and drained

4 large slices dense wholegrain bread

2 gherkins (pickles), thinly sliced

1. Put the tuna in a small bowl with the carrot, spring onion and mayonnaise and mix.

2. Divide the lettuce leaves between two slices of bread. Top with the tuna and mayonnaise mixture and the gherkins.

3. Top with the two remaining bread slices.

**Note:** Wholegrain breads have a high fibre content and contain a combination of healthy grains and seeds.

# tuna, caper and bean sandwich

100 g (3¹/₂ oz) tinned tuna in spring water, drained

1 teaspoon finely chopped drained, rinsed capers in brine

3 teaspoons low-fat mayonnaise

1 tablespoon canned cannellini beans, mashed

200 g (7 oz) baby English spinach leaves

1 large tomato, sliced

4 slices wholemeal (whole-wheat) sourdough bread

1 Put the tuna, capers, mayonnaise and cannellini beans in a bowl and mix.

2 Spread the tuna mixture over two of the bread slices. Top with the spinach leaves and tomato. Top with the remaining bread slices.

**Note:** Kids like what they know, so if they only ever get to know white bread that is all they will ever want. Offer a wide range of breads like rye, wholemeal (whole-wheat), wholegrain and pitta pockets.

# chicken, tomato and avo sandwich

## SERVES 2

1 tablespoon olive oil

1 skinless chicken breast fillet, cut in half horizontally

1 tablespoon lemon juice

2 pieces ciabatta or Turkish bread, cut in half horizontally

low-fat mayonnaise, to serve

1/2 avocado, sliced

1 tomato, sliced

1 handful of rocket (arugula) leaves

Heat the oil in a frying pan over medium heat. Add the chicken and cook on both sides for 2–3 minutes, or until cooked through. Sprinkle with the lemon juice, then take out of the pan.

Spread the bread with the mayonnaise.

Put a piece of chicken on two of the bread pieces. Layer two of the bread pieces with the rocket, tomato, chicken and avocado. Top with the bread, then serve.

# lamb pide with chickpea spread

2 trimmed lamb fillets

2 teaspoons lemon juice

2 teaspoons ground cumin

2 teaspoons olive oil

2 pieces Turkish bread, halved

1 tomato, sliced

1 small handful rocket (arugula) leaves

**chickpea spread**

50 g (1³/₄ oz) drained canned chickpeas

1 teaspoon lemon juice

2 teaspoons low-fat plain yoghurt

1. Marinate the lamb fillets in the lemon juice, ground cumin, olive oil and some salt and pepper.

2. Process the chickpeas, lemon juice and yoghurt in a food processor.

3. Cook the lamb in a frying pan over medium heat for 3 minutes on each side, or until done to your liking.

4. Spread the bread with the chickpea spread. Top with thin slices of lamb, tomato and rocket leaves.

# lentil, corn and salad wraps

MAKES 4

200 g (7 oz) tinned brown lentils, rinsed and drained

200 g (7 oz) tinned corn kernels, rinsed and drained

2 ripe tomatoes, seeded and finely chopped

½ small red onion, finely chopped

½ red capsicum (pepper), seeded and finely chopped

½ green capsicum (pepper), seeded and finely chopped

1 handful flat-leaf (Italian) parsley, chopped

2 tablespoons low-fat mayonnaise dressing

4 lavash or other unleavened breads

60 g (2¼ oz) reduced-fat smooth ricotta

1 handful baby rocket (arugula) or baby English spinach leaves

1 Put the lentils in a large bowl and mash with a fork. Mix in the corn, vegetables and parsley. Stir through the mayonnaise.

2 Spread the breads with the ricotta, then divide the lentil salad and rocket or baby spinach leaves among the breads.

3 Roll up each bread to enclose the filling. Wrap in baking paper or plastic wrap to secure.

# chicken and tzatziki wrap

**tzatziki**

1/2 telegraph (long) cucumber

100 g (3 1/2 oz) low-fat natural yoghurt

1/4 teaspoon lemon juice

1 tablespoon chopped mint

2 skinless chicken thigh fillets, trimmed

2 sheets of lavash or other flat bread

2 large butter lettuce leaves

1. To make the tzatziki, seed and grate the cucumber into a bowl, then sprinkle with 1/2 teaspoon salt. Leave for 10 minutes. Drain, then mix with the yoghurt, lemon juice mint.

2. Cook the chicken in a frying pan over medium heat for 5–7 minutes on each side.

3. Place a large butter lettuce leaf on each piece of lavash. Spread with some of the tzatziki. Top with a sliced chicken fillet. Roll up, folding one end closed.

# chicken pocket cones

**MAKES 4**

1 small pitta bread round

1 tablespoon cheese spread

1 tablespoon low-fat mayonnaise

4 slices chicken loaf, halved

chives, for tying cones

1 small Lebanese (short) cucumber, cut into small sticks

4 lettuce leaves, shredded

1 small tomato, finely chopped

1 Cut the pitta bread in half. Split the halves to make two semi-circles. Spread evenly with the cheese spread and the mayonnaise. Top each with a piece of chicken loaf.

2 Roll each semi-circle into a cone. Tie with a chive to hold the shape.

3 Stuff cones with a few cucumber sticks, some lettuce and top with the tomato. Refrigerate for at least 1 hour before serving.

# ham, cottage cheese and tomato

### MAKES 2

2 bagels

50 g (1³/₄ oz) low-fat cottage cheese

1 tablespoon finely shredded basil

1 tablespoon Dijon mustard

100 g (3¹/₂ oz) shaved light ham

1 large handful baby English spinach leaves

1 large tomato, sliced

1. Cut the bagels in half.

2. Combine the cottage cheese and basil.

3. Spread the bagel bases lightly with the mustard, then top with the cottage cheese mixture, ham, spinach and tomato.

# ham, cheese and cucumber on sourdough

2 tablespoons ready-made tomato chutney

1 tablespoon low-fat plain yoghurt

4 slices sourdough bread

2 slices low-fat cheddar cheese

50 g (1¾ oz) shaved light ham

½ Lebanese (short) cucumber

1 small handful snow pea (mangetout) sprouts

1. Combine the ready-made tomato chutney with the yoghurt.

2. Spread onto two slices of sourdough bread. Top each with a slices of cheese, then the light ham.

3. Use a potato peeler to shred the cucumber and divide among the sandwiches.

4. Top each with a handful of snow pea sprouts and another slice of sourdough bread.

# tuna, avocado and cheese wraps

### MAKES 2

95 g (3¼ oz) tinned sandwich tuna in spring water, drained

2 tortillas

1 tablespoon low-fat mayonnaise

1 small handful rocket (arugula) leaves

½ small avocado, thinly sliced

4 tablespoon grated low-fat cheddar cheese

1 Put the drained tuna in a bowl and finely flake with a fork.

2 Spread the tortillas evenly with the mayonnaise, then top half of each tortilla with the rocket, flaked tuna, avocado slices and cheese.

3 Roll up, starting from the filled side, to enclose the filling. Cut in half to serve.

# chicken club sandwich

## MAKES 2

½ barbecued chicken

4 bacon slices

4 tablespoons low-fat mayonnaise

2 tablespoons wholegrain mustard

4 slices rye bread

½ avocado, sliced

2 lettuce leaves

1 tomato, sliced

1 Remove the meat from the chicken bones and shred. Discard the skin.

2 Fry the bacon until crisp and brown. Drain on paper towels.

3 Combine the mayonnaise and mustard in a bowl.

4 Spread two slices of the bread with the mayonnaise mixture. Top with the avocado, lettuce and tomato.

5 Top with the shredded chicken and bacon. Top with the remaining bread slices.

# B.L.T. with cheese

2 slices bacon

4 thick slices white bread

2 slices low-fat cheddar cheese

2 cos (romaine) lettuce leaves, shredded

1 small tomato, thinly sliced

1 tablespoon tomato sauce or
low-fat mayonnaise

1  Cook the bacon under a preheated grill (broiler) for 2–3 minutes on each side.

2  Put the cheese on two slices of bread. Top with lettuce, tomato and the bacon.

3  Drizzle with tomato sauce. Top with the remaining slices of bread.

# chicken nugget pockets

**MAKES 2**

2 pitta pocket breads

2 tablespoons low-fat mayonnaise

2 large lettuce leaves, shredded

2 tablespoons corn relish

6 chicken nuggets

1 Carefully split the pocket breads open.

2 Spread the mayonnaise on the inside of the bread.

3 Fill the bread pockets with lettuce. Spoon the relish over.

4 Grill (broil) the chicken nuggets for 3 minutes. on each side. Leave to cool.

5 Put the nuggets into the pockets and wrap with baking paper to hold.

# chickpea patties with green salad

330 g (11³/₄ oz/1¹/₂ cups) tinned chickpeas, drained

2 tablespoons low-fat natural yoghurt

2 teaspoons chopped flat-leaf (Italian) parsley

¹/₄ teaspoon garlic powder

2 spring onions (scallions), chopped

2 tablespoons cornflake crumbs

2 teaspoons oil

mixed green salad, to serve

2 wholemeal pitta or pocket breads

1. Put the chickpeas in a food processor with the yoghurt. Process until smooth, then put in a bowl.

2. Add the parsley, garlic powder and spring onion. Divide the mixture into four patties. Roll in the cornflake crumbs.

3. Heat the oil in a frying pan over medium heat. Cook the patties for 2–3 minutes on each side, or until golden brown. Drain on paper towels. Leave to cool completely.

4. Pack the patties into an airtight container with some mixed salad and pitta bread.

**Note:** Wrap the bread separately to help keep it fresh.

# leek, zucchini and cheese frittata

**SERVES 4**

2 tablespoons olive oil

3 leeks, thinly sliced (white part only)

2 zucchini (courgettes), cut into matchstick pieces

1 garlic clove, crushed

5 eggs, lightly beaten

4 tablespoons freshly grated parmesan cheese

4 tablespoons diced Swiss cheese

1   Heat 1 tablespoon of the olive oil in a small ovenproof pan. Add the leek and cook, stirring, over low heat until slightly softened. Cover and cook the leek for 10 minutes, stirring occasionally.

2   Add the zucchini and garlic and cook for another 10 minutes. Transfer the mixture to a bowl. Allow to cool.

3   Add the egg and cheeses to the zucchini mixture and stir through. Heat the remaining oil in the pan, then add the egg mixture and smooth the surface. Cook over low heat for 15 minutes, or until the frittata is almost set.

4   Put the pan under a preheated hot grill (broiler) for 3–5 minutes, or until the top is set and golden. Allow the frittata to stand for 5 minutes before cutting into wedges and serving. Serve with a fresh green salad.

# bean enchiladas

2 teaspoons light olive oil

½ onion, thinly sliced

1 garlic clove, crushed

1 teaspoon ground cumin

3 tablespoons salt-reduced vegetable stock

2 tomatoes, peeled, deseeded and chopped

2 teaspoons tomato paste (concentrated purée)

425 g (15 oz) tinned three-bean mix, drained and rinsed

1 tablespoon chopped coriander (cilantro) leaves

4 flour tortillas

½ small avocado, chopped

60 g (2¼ oz) light sour cream

1 small handful coriander (cilantro) sprigs

60 g (2¼ oz) shredded lettuce

Preheat the oven to 170°C (325°F/Gas 3).

Heat the oil in a frying pan over medium heat. Add the onion and cook for 3–4 minutes, or until just soft. Add the garlic and cook for a further 30 seconds.

Add the cumin, vegetable stock, tomato and tomato paste and cook for 6–8 minutes, or until thick.

Add the beans to the sauce and cook for 5 minutes, then add the coriander.

Meanwhile, wrap the tortillas in foil and warm in the oven for 3–4 minutes.

Place a tortilla on a plate and spread with a large scoop of the bean mixture.

Top with some avocado, sour cream, coriander sprigs and lettuce. Roll the enchiladas up, tucking in the ends. Cut each one in half to serve.

# sushi hand rolls

**MAKES 35**

200 g (7 oz/1 cup) sushi rice

2 tablespoons white rice vinegar

1 tablespoon sugar

10 nori sheets, cut into quarters

sliced cucumber, pickled daikon, sliced avocado and blanched English spinach, to fill

1 Put the rice in a saucepan with 310 ml (10¾ fl oz/ 1¼ cups) of water and bring to the boil. Simmer, covered, over very low heat for 12 minutes, or until the water is absorbed. Remove from the heat. Leave for 15 minutes.

2 Mix the white rice vinegar, sugar and a pinch of salt, then stir through the rice. Leave to cool.

3 Cut the nori sheets into quarters.

4 Put 1½ tablespoons of rice in the middle of each nori square.

5 Top with 2–3 fillings from a selection of the fillings. Roll into a cone shape and serve with Japanese soy sauce for dipping.

**Note:** If you are making these rolls to eat at home, you can add fillings like sliced sashimi tuna, cooked prawns (shrimp), and fresh or smoked salmon. Don't pack these fillings in lunchboxes, for food safety reasons.

# mixed pasta salad

SERVES 2

100 g (3¹/₂ oz/¹/₂ cup) mixed pasta twists

100 g (3¹/₂ oz) cooked skinless chicken breast, cubed

1 small carrot, grated

1 small zucchini (courgette), grated

1 spring onion (scallion), chopped

¹/₂ small red capsicum (pepper)

130 g (4³/₄ oz) tinned creamed corn

3 lettuce leaves

3 small tomato wedges

1 wholemeal pitta or pocket bread

1   Cook the pasta in boiling water for 10–12 minutes, or until tender. Drain, then leave to cool.

2   Combine the pasta with the chicken, carrot, zucchini, onion, capsicum and corn.

3   Put the lettuce in the bottom of an airtight container. Spoon the chicken mixture onto the lettuce. Top with tomato wedges.

# vegetable and bean salad

## SERVES 2

310 g (11 oz) tinned four-bean mix

6 green beans

1 zucchini (courgette), sliced

4 cherry tomatoes, halved

1 small pickling onion, sliced

1 tablespoon light salad dressing

1 tablespoon chopped flat-leaf (Italian) parsley

2 wholegrain bread rolls

1 Drain the beans and rinse well. Put in a bowl.

2 Cut the green beans into 3 cm (1¼ inch) pieces. Cook the green beans and zucchini in boiling water until tender. Drain and cool in cold water.

3 Add the cooked vegetables to the beans with the tomatoes, onion and dressing. Mix well.

4 Wrap the bread separately to keep fresh.

**Note:** Four-bean mix consists of red kidney beans, garbanzo beans and butterbeans (lima beans).

# brown rice salad

## SERVES 1

210 g (7½ oz/1 cup) cooked brown rice

1 slice lean ham, chopped

50 g (1¾ oz/⅓ cup) cooked peas

1 small carrot, grated

1 spring onion (scallion), chopped

1 teaspoon oil

3 teaspoons white wine vinegar

2 teaspoons chopped chives

1. Combine the rice, ham, peas, carrot, spring onion, oil, vinegar and chives in a bowl.

2. Put in an airtight lunchbox.

# chef's salad

## SERVES 2

2 slices Swiss cheese, cut into strips

2 slices leg ham, cut into strips

45 g (1½ oz/¼ cup) cooked chicken

4 cherry tomatoes, quartered

1 hard-boiled egg, diced

2 lettuce leaf cups

1 tablespoon light French dressing

1. Combine the cheese, ham, chicken, tomato, and egg in a bowl.

2. Serve the salad in the lettuce cups in an airtight container. Drizzle the dressing over the salad.

**Variation:** You can also use turkey instead of chicken.

# nicoise salad

### SERVES 2

3 tablespoons olive oil

1 tablespoon white wine vinegar

1/2 garlic clove, crushed

160 g (5³/4 oz) iceberg lettuce, shredded

6 cherry tomatoes, cut into quarters

90 g (3¹/4 oz) baby green beans, trimmed and blanched

1/2 small red capsicum (pepper), deseeded and thinly sliced

1/2 celery stalk, cut into 5 cm (2 inch) strips

1/2 Lebanese (short) cucumber, deseeded, cut into 5 cm (2 inch) strips

180 g (6¹/2 oz) tinned tuna, drained and flaked

1 egg, boiled, quartered

6 stoned kalamata olives, halved (optional)

2 anchovy fillets, finely chopped (optional)

1 Combine the oil, vinegar and garlic in a small bowl.

2 Put the lettuce, tomato, beans, capsicum, celery, cucumber, tuna, olives and anchovies in a large bowl.

3 Pour the dressing over and toss. Serve the salad topped with the egg quarters. Add olives and anchovies if desired.

**Note:** Tinned tuna is a tasty, nutritious food, rich in the omega-3 fats that are such good brain food for growing children. The best choices are those packed in a good oil (such as olive, canola or sunflower oil) or spring water.

# couscous salad

150 g (5½ oz) orange sweet potato, cubed

50 g (1¾ oz) green beans, halved

175 g (6 oz) instant couscous

250 ml (9 fl oz/1 cup) boiling reduced-salt chicken stock

100 g (3½ oz) cherry tomatoes, halved

75 g (2½ oz) frozen corn kernels, thawed

75 g (2½ oz) frozen peas, thawed

½ red capsicum (pepper), chopped

30 g (1 oz) chopped flat-leaf (Italian) parsley

10 g (¼ oz) chopped mint

**dressing**

½ garlic clove, crushed

1 tablespoon lemon juice

2 teaspoons olive oil

½ teaspoon honey

¼ teaspoon wholegrain mustard

1. Boil or steam the sweet potato and beans in separate saucepans until tender, then drain.

2. Put the couscous in a large bowl. Pour the boiling stock over the couscous. Cover and leave for 5 minutes, or until all the liquid has been absorbed. Fluff with a fork to separate the grains.

3. Add the sweet potato, beans, tomato, corn, peas, capsicum and herbs to the couscous and mix.

4. Whisk together the garlic, lemon juice, oil, honey and mustard in a bowl. Pour the dressing over the salad and toss.

# mixed salad

4 button mushrooms, thinly sliced

½ tablespoon chopped flat-leaf (Italian) parsley

1 teaspoon lemon juice

1 tablespoon oil

2 small zucchini (courgettes), thinly sliced

½ green capsicum (pepper), finely chopped

2 small tomatoes, chopped into small pieces

a few mint leaves, finely chopped

1½ tablespoons light French dressing

1. Put the mushrooms in a bowl and add the parsley, lemon juice and oil.

2. Boil the zucchini in a saucepan over medium heat for 1 minute. Drain well and rinse in cold water. Drain again.

3. Put the capsicum, tomato and mint in a bowl. Add the mushrooms. Pour the dressing over and mix.

# light chicken caesar salad

### SERVES 2

2 thick slices wholemeal (whole-wheat) or
wholegrain bread

oil spray

25 g (1 oz) bacon slices, thinly sliced

½ cos (romaine) lettuce, outer leaves and
core removed

1 cooked chicken breast fillet, sliced

2 anchovy fillets, drained, rinsed and halved
lengthways

15 g (½ oz) shredded parmesan cheese

1 tablespoon finely chopped flat-leaf (Italian)
parsley

**low-fat dressing**

60 g (2¼ oz) low-fat plain yoghurt

1½ tablespoons low-fat mayonnaise
dressing

2 teaspoons Dijon mustard

2 teaspoons lemon juice

¼ teaspoon Worcestershire sauce

1  Preheat the oven to 180°C (350°F/Gas 4). Remove the crusts from the bread and cut into 1 cm (½ inch) cubes. Place on a tray. Bake for 12 minutes, or until lightly browned.

2  Lightly spray a small frying pan with oil. Cook the bacon over medium heat for 2 minutes, or until cooked. Drain on paper towels.

3  Combine the dressing ingredients in a bowl.

4  Break the lettuce leaves into smaller pieces. Add the chicken, bread, bacon, half of the anchovies, and parmesan.

5  Toss through two-thirds of the dressing. Scatter over the remaining anchovies, parsley and parmesan. Drizzle over the remaining dressing.

**Hint:** You can use poached or barbecued chicken breast in this recipe. Remove any skin and fat.

# vegetable and noodle stir-fry

**SERVES 2**

60 g (2¼ oz) cellophane or egg noodles

1 teaspoon oil

½ carrot, cut into sticks

½ celery stalk, chopped

½ small zucchini (courgette), halved
lengthways, sliced

½ red capsicum (pepper), deseeded,
cut into sticks

40 g (1½ oz) cauliflower florets

40 g (1½ oz) broccoli florets

30 g (1 oz) green beans, sliced

½ garlic clove, crushed

1 tablespoon salt-reduced soy sauce

1. Put the noodles in a bowl. Cover with boiling water. Leave to stand for 1 minute, or until tender. Drain.

2. Heat the oil in a wok or frying pan. Add the carrot, celery, zucchini, capsicum, cauliflower, broccoli, beans and garlic and stir-fry for 4–5 minutes.

3. Toss the noodles through the vegetables with the soy sauce. Stir-fry for another minute.

# hokkien noodle salad

**SERVES 2**

225 g (8 oz) hokkien noodles

100 g (3½ oz) broccoli, cut into florets

2 spring onions (scallions), sliced

½ red capsicum (pepper), thinly sliced

½ green capsicum (pepper), thinly sliced

½ carrot, thinly sliced

50 g (1¾ oz) snow peas, sliced

50 g (1¾ oz) baby corn, halved lengthways

3 tablespoons chopped coriander (cilantro) leaves

½ teaspoon sesame oil

1½ tablespoons sweet chilli sauce

1½ tablespoons light soy sauce

1 tablespoon lime juice

1. Gently separate the noodles and put in a heatproof bowl. Cover with boiling water. Leave to stand for 2 minutes, then rinse under cold water. Drain well.

2. Boil or steam the broccoli for 3 minutes, or until bright green and tender. Rinse under cold water and drain.

3. Combine the noodles, vegetables and coriander in a large bowl.

4. Combine the sesame oil, sweet chilli sauce, soy sauce and lime juice. Pour over the salad and toss to coat.

# pasta with chicken and asparagus

## SERVES 2

2 tablespoons canola oil

2 small skinless chicken breast fillets, sliced

½ small leek, halved lengthways, thinly sliced

1 garlic clove, crushed

75 g (2½ oz) green beans, diagonally sliced into 3 cm (1¼ inch) pieces

75 g (2½ oz) asparagus, trimmed and sliced into 3 cm (1¼ inch) pieces

125 ml (4 fl oz/½ cup) chicken stock

150 g (5½ oz) pasta (we used large spiral pasta)

1   Heat 1 tablespoon of the oil in a large non-stick frying pan over medium heat. Cook the chicken for 4 minutes on each side, or until cooked through.

2   Heat the remaining oil in the pan. Add the leek and cook, stirring often, for 6–7 minutes or until almost soft. Add the garlic, beans and asparagus.

3   Cook for 2–3 minutes, or until the vegetables are tender. Increase the heat to high and pour in the stock. Simmer for 2–3 minutes, or until the liquid reduces slightly.

4   Meanwhile, cook the pasta in a large saucepan of boiling water for 12 minutes, or until just tender. Drain and return to the pan.

5   Add the chicken to the pasta along with the vegetables and sauce and toss.

# penne with vegetables

**SERVES 3**

250 g (9 oz) penne

1½ tablespoons olive oil

2 small zucchini (courgettes), sliced

1 garlic clove, crushed

1 spring onion (scallion), chopped

½ red capsicum (pepper), cut into strips

30 g (1 oz) corn kernels

1 tomato, chopped

1 tablespoon chopped flat-leaf (Italian) parsley

1. Cook the penne in a large saucepan of boiling water for 12 minutes or until just tender. Drain, then return to the pan.

2. Heat 1 tablespoon of the oil in a large frying pan. Add the zucchini and cook, stirring, for 3 minutes.

3. Add the garlic, spring onion, capsicum and corn. Stir-fry for another 2–3 minutes.

4. Stir the tomato into the vegetable mixture and set aside.

5. Add the parsley and the remaining oil to the pasta and toss. Top with the vegetables

# tomato, tuna and white bean pasta

### SERVES 2

50 g (1³/₄ oz) small bow-tie or other small pasta

90 g (3¹/₄ oz/¹/₃ cup) chunky tomato-based pasta sauce

100 g (3¹/₂ oz) tinned tuna in spring water, drained

2 tablespoons drained, rinsed tinned cannellini beans

1 teaspoon chopped drained, rinsed capers in brine

1 teaspoon finely chopped basil

1 Cook the pasta in a large saucepan of boiling water for 12 minutes or until just tender. Drain, then return to the pan.

2 Put the pasta sauce, tuna, beans, capers and basil in a small saucepan. Stir over medium heat for 1–2 minutes, or until heated through. Toss through the pasta.

# spiral pasta with broccoli and ham

## SERVES 2

200 g (7 oz) spiral pasta

125 g (4½ oz) broccoli florets

15 g (½ oz) butter

125 g (4½ oz) leg ham, cut into strips

1 garlic clove, crushed

3 spring onions (scallions), chopped

100 g (3½ oz) mushrooms, sliced

125 ml (4 fl oz/½ cup) thick (double/heavy) cream

1 small handful flat-leaf (Italian) parsley, roughly chopped

1 Cook the pasta in a large saucepan of boiling water for 12 minutes or until just tender. Drain, then return to the pan.

2 Cook the broccoli in a small saucepan of rapidly boiling water for 2 minutes or until tender. Drain.

3 Heat butter in a large frying pan. Add the ham and stir over medium heat for 2 minutes, or until browned.

4 Add garlic, spring onion and mushrooms and stir for 2 minutes. Add drained pasta, broccoli, cream and parsley. Stir for 1 minute, or until heated through.

**Variation:** Add some cooked peas or diced, cooked carrots.

# vegetable couscous

### SERVES 4

15 g (½ oz) unsalted butter

½ onion, sliced

½ garlic clove, crushed

½ teaspoon ground cumin

1 carrot, thinly sliced

75 g (2½ oz) pumpkin (winter squash), chopped

150 g (5½ oz) tinned chickpeas, drained

200 g (7 oz) tinned chopped tomatoes

½ all-purpose potato, chopped

1 small eggplant (aubergine), chopped

1½ tablespoons vegetable stock

75 g (2½ oz) green beans, cut into short lengths

1 zucchini (courgette), cut into chunks

**COUSCOUS**

125 ml (4 fl oz/½ cup) salt-reduced vegetable stock

90 g (3¼ oz) instant couscous

15 g (½ oz) unsalted butter

1 Melt the butter in a saucepan over medium heat. Add the onion, garlic and cumin and cook for 2–3 minutes, or until softened.

2 Add the carrot, pumpkin, chickpeas, tomato, potato, eggplant and vegetable stock. Cook for 10 minutes, stirring occasionally.

3 Add the beans and zucchini and cook for another 5 minutes, or until the vegetables are tender.

4 To make the couscous, pour the stock into a saucepan and add 3 tablespoons of water. Bring to the boil. Remove from the heat and stir in the couscous and butter. Cover and stand for 5 minutes. Fluff the grains with a fork.

5 Fold the vegetables through the couscous.

# afternoon treats

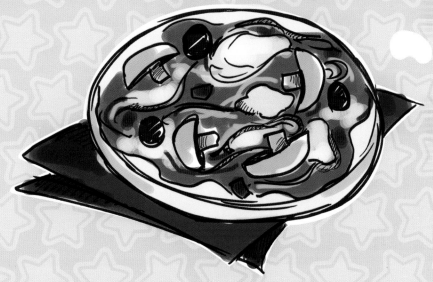

# creamy chicken and corn soup

**SERVES 6**

1 litre (35 fl oz/4 cups) salt-reduced chicken stock

40 g (1¹/₂ oz/¹/₂ cup) small pasta

175 g (6 oz/1 cup) finely chopped cooked chicken (see Hint)

125 g (4¹/₂ oz/¹/₂ cup) tinned creamed corn

1 tablespoon chopped flat-leaf (Italian) parsley

1  Put the stock and pasta in a saucepan. Bring to the boil, then reduce the heat and simmer for 10–12 minutes, or until tender.

2  Add the chicken and corn and simmer for 5 minutes.

3  Stir in the parsley and cool slightly. Process in a blender or food processor until smooth. Reheat to serve.

**Hint:** Use skinless barbecued (grilled) chicken or cooked chicken breast, sliced.

# potato and pumpkin soup

**SERVES 4**

1 tablespoon canola oil

1 leek, halved lengthways, washed and sliced

2 garlic cloves, peeled and crushed

500 g (1 lb 2 oz) white-skinned potatoes, peeled and chopped

500 g (1 lb 2 oz) butternut pumpkin (squash), peeled, deseeded and chopped

1 litre (35 fl oz/4 cups) vegetable stock

finely chopped chives, to serve

sour cream, to serve (optional)

1  Heat the oil in a saucepan over medium heat. Add the leek and garlic and cook, stirring, for 2 minutes. Reduce the heat to low. Cover the pan with a lid and cook, stirring occasionally, for 8 minutes, or until the leek is very soft.

2  Add the potato, pumpkin and stock to the pan. Bring to the boil. Reduce the heat and simmer for about 20 minutes, or until the vegetables are very soft. Set aside to cool slightly.

3  Purée the soup in a blender or food processor until smooth. Reheat to serve.

# minestrone

### SERVES 20

2 tablespoons olive oil

1 onion, chopped

1 bacon slice, finely chopped

3 carrots, halved lengthways and chopped

3 zucchini (courgettes), halved lengthways and chopped

2 celery stalks, sliced

2 all-purpose potatoes, chopped

400 g (14 oz) tinned diced tomatoes

300 g (10½ oz/1½ cups) tinned four-bean mix, drained and rinsed

30 g (1 oz/⅓ cup) small pasta shapes

125 g (4½ oz/1 cup) green beans, trimmed and sliced

grated parmesan cheese, to serve

chopped flat-leaf (Italian) parsley, to serve

1   Heat the oil in a large saucepan and cook the onion and bacon until the onion is soft.

2   Add the carrot, zucchini, celery, potatoes, tomatoes and four-bean mix. Cook, stirring, for 1 minute.

3   Add 2.5 litres (87 fl oz/10 cups) of water to the pan. Bring to the boil, then reduce the heat and simmer, covered, for 1 hour.

4   Stir in the pasta and green beans. Simmer for 12 minutes, or until tender.

5   Sprinkle the minestrone with parmesan cheese and chopped parsley and serve with crusty bread.

**Note:** Prepare this recipe ahead of time and keep it in the refrigerator for warming winter after-school meals through the week or on weekends.

# pea and ham soup

### SERVES 4–6

2 tablespoons olive oil

2 onions, finely chopped

2 carrots, diced

2 celery sticks, diced

1 small turnip, finely chopped

440g (15½ oz) split green peas, rinsed and drained

1 smoked ham hock (800g/1 lb 12 oz)

2 bay leaves

2 sprigs thyme

½ teaspoon ground ginger

1   Heat the oil in a large saucepan over low heat. Add the onion, carrot, celery and turnip and cook for 5–6 minutes, or until softened.

2   Add the split peas, ham hock, bay leaves, thyme, ground ginger and 2.5 litres (87 fl oz/10 cups) of water. Bring to the boil over medium heat.

3   Reduce the heat and simmer, covered, for 2 hours 30 minutes to 3 hours.

4   Remove the ham bones and meat, then cut the meat into smaller pieces. Return to the soup.

5   Remove the bay leaves and thyme.

# oven chips

### SERVES 6

6 all-purpose potatoes

3 tablespoons olive oil

1. Preheat the oven to 220°C (425°F/Gas 7). Cut the potatoes into slices about 1 cm (1/2 inch) thick.

2. Soak the chips (fries) in cold water for 10 minutes. Drain well, then pat dry with paper towels.

3. Spread the chips onto a baking tray and sprinkle the oil over them. Toss to coat.

4. Bake for 45–55 minutes until golden and crisp, turning occasionally.

# oven-baked chicken nuggets

### SERVES 4

90 g (3¼ oz) cornflakes

400 g (14 oz) chicken breast fillets, cut into bite-sized pieces

2 egg whites, lightly beaten

canola spray

1. Preheat the oven to 200°C (400°F/Gas 6). Lightly spray a baking tray with canola spray.

2. Put the cornflakes in a food processor and process until the mixture forms fine crumbs. Put in a bowl.

3. Toss the chicken pieces in the seasoned flour, then in the egg white. Roll each piece in the crumbs until well coated.

4. Put the nuggets on the baking tray. Bake for 10–12 minutes, or until lightly browned.

# jacket potatoes

MAKES 4

4 large potatoes

**avocado, tomato and corn salsa filling**

2 tomatoes, chopped

125 g (4½ oz) tinned corn kernels

2 spring onions (scallions), chopped

1 tablespoon lime juice

½ teaspoon sugar

1 avocado, diced

1 small handful coriander (cilantro) leaves, chopped

1 tablespoon low-fat sour cream

**mushroom and bacon filling**

3 bacon slices, finely sliced

2 spring onions (scallions), chopped

1 garlic clove, crushed

1 teaspoon chopped thyme

180 g (6 oz/2 cups) sliced button mushrooms

185 g (6½ oz/¾ cup) low-fat sour cream

2 tablespoons chopped flat-leaf (Italian) parsley

grated low-fat cheese, to serve

1. Preheat the oven to 210°C (415°F/Gas 6–7). Pierce potatoes all over with a fork. Put the potatoes on an oven rack. Bake for 1 hour, or until tender.

2. Cut a cross in the top of each potato and squeeze gently to open (you may need to hold the hot potatoes in a clean tea towel as you do this).

3. To make the avocado salsa filling, put the tomatoes, corn kernels, spring onions, lime juice and sugar in a bowl. Mix well, then add the avocado and coriander leaves. Spoon over the baked potatoes, along with some sour cream, if desired.

4. To make the mushroom filling, cook the bacon in a frying pan over medium heat until lightly golden. Add the spring onions, garlic clove, thyme and button mushrooms. Cook for 3–4 minutes over high heat. Add the sour cream. Reduce the heat to low and cook for another minute. Add the parsley, then spoon the mixture over the baked potatoes. Sprinkle with grated cheese.

# ham and pineapple pinwheels

## MAKES ABOUT 24

2 sheets ready-rolled puff pastry

1 egg, lightly beaten

100 g (3½ oz) ham, thinly sliced

150 g (5½ oz) tinned crushed pineapple, well drained

40 g (1½ oz/⅓ cup) grated cheddar cheese

1 Preheat oven to 180°C (350°F/Gas 4). Lightly grease two large baking trays.

2 Lay out the pastry sheets. Brush with the beaten egg.

3 Sprinkle with the ham, pineapple and cheese.

4 Roll each sheet up firmly and evenly. Using a sharp serrated knife, cut each roll into 12 rounds.

5 Place the wheels on the baking trays. Bake for 15 minutes, or until golden and puffed. Serve warm or hot.

**Note:** This recipe can be made up to 3 weeks in advance and stored in freezer.

# crunchy cheese bites

**MAKES ABOUT 26**

250 g (9 oz/2 cups) grated cheddar cheese

125 g (4$\frac{1}{2}$ oz) feta cheese, crumbled

60 g (2$\frac{1}{4}$ oz/$\frac{1}{4}$ cup) ricotta cheese

30 g (1 oz/$\frac{1}{4}$ cup) chopped spring onions (scallions)

1 small tomato, chopped

1 egg, beaten

5 sheets ready-rolled puff pastry

beaten egg, to brush

milk, to brush

1 Preheat the oven to 220°C (425°F/ Gas 7). Combine the cheeses, spring onion, tomato and egg in a bowl.

2 Cut the pastry into circles using a 10 cm (4 inch) cutter. Place heaped teaspoons of the mixture onto one half of each round.

3 Fold the pastry over the filling to make semi-circles. Brush the edges between the pastry with a little of the beaten egg and press the edges together firmly with a fork to seal.

4 Place on a baking tray and brush with a little milk. Bake in the oven for 10–15 minutes, or until puffed and golden. Allow the pastries to cool for at least 10 minutes before serving

# grilled ham, spinach and tomato sandwiches

**SERVES 2**

4 slices bread

1 large ripe tomato, sliced

100 g (3½ oz) shaved low-fat ham

30 g (1oz) baby English spinach

2 slices low-fat tasty cheese

oil spray

1 Top two of the slices of bread with the tomato, ham, spinach and cheese. Cover with the remaining two slices of bread.

2 Spray a sandwich grill or toasted sandwich maker with oil. Cook each sandwich for 3 minutes, or until crisp and golden.

# cheese and ham subs

**MAKES 4**

2 hot dog rolls

215 g (7½ oz) tinned spaghetti in tomato and
cheese sauce

50 g (1¾ oz) sliced ham, chopped

50 g (1¾ oz) cheddar cheese slices, cut
into strips

1 Preheat oven to 180°C (350°F/Gas 4).
Lightly grease a baking tray.

2 Cut the rolls in half horizontally and
place on the tray.

3 Top each roll half with spaghetti,
ham and cheese. Bake 12 minutes, or
until the cheese melts and the bread
is crispy.

# chicken, corn and avocado melt

**SERVES 2–4**

4 thick slices bread

130 g (4¾ oz) tinned creamed corn

8 slices smoked chicken breast

1 avocado, sliced

2 teaspoons chopped chives

90 g (3¼ oz/¾ cup) grated cheddar cheese

1 Preheat the grill (broiler) to hot. Toast the bread lightly on both sides.

2 Spread the creamed corn onto each slice. Top with the chicken and avocado. Sprinkle with the chives and cheese.

3 Place under the grill and cook for 2 minutes, or until cheese is melted and bubbling. Serve immediately.

# mini shepherd's pies

MAKES 4

1 tablespoon oil

500 g (1 lb 2 oz) minced (ground) steak

2 tablespoons plain (all-purpose) flour

250 ml (9 fl oz/1 cup) salt-reduced beef stock

2 tablespoons chopped flat-leaf (Italian) parsley

4 all-purpose potatoes, cooked

3 tablespoons milk

15 g (1/2 oz) unsalted butter

135 g (4³/4 oz/1 cup) frozen mixed vegetables (peas, beans, carrots), thawed

60 g (2¹/4 oz/1/2 cup) grated cheese

3 tablespoons dried breadcrumbs

1   Preheat the oven to 180°C (350°F/Gas 4). Heat the oil in a frying pan over medium heat. Add the meat and brown, breaking the meat up with a spoon.

2   Stir in the flour and cook, stirring, for 1 minute.

3   Blend in the stock and parsley. Simmer, stirring, for about 5 minutes, or until the mixture thickens.

4   Mash the potatoes well. Add the milk and butter and beat until smooth, adding more of each if needed.

5   Spoon the meat mixture into four 200 ml (7 fl oz) ovenproof bowls.

6   Top with the mixed vegetables and spread the mashed potato over the top.

7   Mix together the cheese and breadcrumbs and sprinkle over each pie. Bake in the oven for 10–15 minutes, or until the tops are golden.

# ratatouille tarts

## MAKES 4 TARTS

2 sheets ready-rolled puff pastry

1 egg, lightly beaten

1 tablespoon olive oil

1 onion, finely sliced

2 garlic cloves, crushed

2 long slender eggplant (aubergine), cut into thin slices

2 zucchini (courgettes), cut into thin slices

1 red capsicum (pepper), diced

2 tomatoes, roughly chopped

1 Preheat oven to 180°C (350°F/Gas 4). Brush one pastry sheet with egg. Top with the other sheet. Cut pastry into 4 squares.

2 Place on a large baking tray and cook for 20 minutes, until puffed and golden. Set aside to cool.

3 Heat the oil in a large heavy-based frying pan. Cook the onion and garlic over medium heat for 5 minutes. Add the eggplant, zucchini and capsicum. Cook, covered, for 10 minutes, stirring occasionally.

4 Add the tomatoes and cook, uncovered, for about 10 minutes, stirring.

5 Cut an 8 cm (3¼ inch) round hole in each of the pastry squares, and pull out the soft pastry in the centre.

6 Fill each of the holes with vegetable mixture.

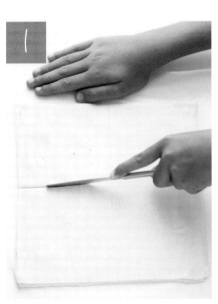

# instant mini pizzas

## MAKES 6

3 English muffins, split in half

unsalted butter

3 tablespoons chunky tomato-based pasta sauce

90 g (3¼ oz) cooked bacon, cut into strips

60 g (2¼ oz/½ cup) grated cheddar cheese

1 Preheat the oven to 240°C (475°F/Gas 8). Lightly spread the muffin halves with butter.

2 Spread the tomato sauce over the muffins. Top with the strips of bacon and the cheese.

3 Place onto a baking tray and bake for 8–10 minutes, or until the cheese has melted.

**Variations:** Use ham or chicken instead of bacon. Add pineapple pieces, avocado chunks or olives before heating in the oven. Small sized pitta bread (pockets) can also be used instead of muffins.

# fish patties

## SERVES 4

2 tablespoons canola oil

500 g (1 lb 2 oz) boneless white fish fillets

1 leek, halved lengthways, washed and chopped

2 garlic cloves, crushed

700 g (1 lb 9 oz) new potatoes, peeled and quartered

30 g (1 oz/¼ cup) chopped spring onions (scallions)

iceberg lettuce leaves, to serve

1. Heat 2 teaspoons of the oil in a large non-stick frying pan over medium heat. Add the fish fillets and cook for 3–4 minutes on each side, or until cooked. Leave to cool.

2. Flake the fish with a fork. Heat another 2 teaspoons of the oil in the same frying pan over medium heat.

3. Cook the leek and garlic, stirring, for 5–6 minutes, or until the leek softens. Set aside.

4. Meanwhile, put the potatoes in a large saucepan. Cover with cold water and bring to the boil. Boil for 15 minutes, or until tender. Drain well. Mash with a potato masher.

5. Combine the mashed potato, flaked fish, leek mixture and spring onions in a large bowl. Shape into eight patties and put on a plate. Cover and chill for 1 hour.

6. Heat the left-over oil in the frying pan over medium heat. Cook the patties for 3–4 minutes on each side, or until light golden. Serve with lettuce.

# quesadillas

**MAKES 4**

1 tablespoon oil

500 g (1 lb 2 oz) minced (ground) chicken

35 g (1¼ oz) packet taco seasoning mix

125 g (4½ oz/½ cup) tomato salsa

230 g (8½ oz/1 cup) tinned refried beans

250 g (9 oz/2 cups) grated low-fat tasty cheese

4 flour tortillas

sour cream, to serve

1. Heat the oil in a frying pan and cook the chicken, using a fork to break up any lumps.

2. Add the taco seasoning and stir, cooking for 2 minutes. Add the salsa. Stir until warmed through. Remove from the heat.

3. In a small saucepan, heat the refried beans with 4 tablespoons of water until the mixture is thick.

4. To make the quesadillas, put some of the cheese on half of each tortilla. Top with the chicken mixture, refried beans and more cheese.

5. Fold the top over and cook each one in a frying pan over medium heat until browned on both sides. Serve with a dollop of sour cream.

# meatballs

**MAKES 25**

375 g (13 oz) minced (ground) beef

1 small onion, finely chopped

40 g (1½ oz/½ cup) fresh breadcrumbs

1 tablespoon tomato paste (concentrated purée)

1 teaspoon worcestershire sauce

1 egg, lightly beaten

2 tablespoons oil

1. Put the beef, onion, breadcrumbs, tomato paste, sauce and egg in a large bowl and mix.

2. Shape level tablespoons of mixture into balls.

3. Heat the oil in a large frying pan. Add the meatballs and cook over medium heat for 10 minutes, or until evenly browned.

4. Drain on paper towels. Serve hot or cold with tomato sauce (ketchup), if desired.

# glazed drumettes

**SERVES 4**

16 chicken drumettes

4 tablespoons golden syrup (dark corn syrup)

3 tablespoons pear juice

1 tablespoon canola oil

1  Put the drumettes in a shallow non-metallic dish. Combine the remaining ingredients and pour over the drumettes. Marinate overnight, turning occasionally.

2  Preheat the oven to 180°C (350°F/Gas 4). Transfer the drumettes and marinade to a baking tin.

3  Bake for 20–25 minutes, turning frequently. Serve hot or cold.

**Note:** Chicken drumettes are available from most supermarkets and chicken shops. They are simply the wing with the tip removed and the flesh scraped back away from the bone and turned inside out.

# rice-crumbed fish pieces

**SERVES 4**

2 eggs

2 tablespoons rice drink

60 g (2¼ oz/½ cup) soy-free, gluten-free plain (all-purpose) flour

70 g (2½ oz/1 cup) rice crumbs

4 x 125 g (4½ oz) boneless white fish fillets, cut into pieces

canola oil spray

iceberg lettuce leaves, to serve

1  Preheat the oven to 220°C (425°F/Gas 7). Line two large baking trays with baking paper.

2  Combine the egg and rice drink in a shallow dish. Put the flour and rice crumbs in two separate shallow dishes.

3  Dip the fish in the flour, then the egg mixture, and then in the rice crumbs to coat well.

4  Lay the crumbed fish in a single layer on one of the lined trays. Spray both sides of the fish lightly with oil.

5  Bake for 20 minutes, turning halfway through, or until the fish is cooked.

# vegetable filo pouches

**SERVES 4**

oil spray

8 sheets filo pastry

80 g (2³/₄ oz/¹/₂ cup) sesame seeds

**filling**

450 g (1 lb/3 cups) grated carrot

2 large onions, finely chopped

1 tablespoon grated fresh ginger

1 tablespoon finely chopped coriander
(cilantro) leaves

225 g (8 oz/1¹/₃ cups) tinned water
chestnuts, rinsed and sliced

1 tablespoon white miso paste

3 tablespoons tahini paste

1. Preheat the oven to 180°C (350°F/ Gas 4). Spray two baking trays with oil.

2. To make the filling, combine the carrot, onion, ginger, coriander and 250 ml (9 fl oz/1 cup) of water in a large pan. Cover and cook over low heat for 20 minutes.

3. Uncover, cook for a further 5 minutes, or until all the liquid has evaporated. Remove from the heat and cool slightly. Stir in the water chestnuts, miso and tahini.

4. Spray one sheet of filo pastry with oil. Top with another three pastry sheets, spraying between each layer.

5. Cut the pastry into six squares. Repeat the process with the remaining pastry sheets.

6. Divide the filling evenly between each square, placing the filling in the centre. Bring the edges together and pinch to form a pouch.

7. Spray each pouch with oil, then press in the sesame seeds. Place on the trays and bake for 10–12 minutes, or until golden brown.

# macaroni cheese

**SERVES 4**

30 g (1 oz) unsalted butter

1 tablespoon plain (all-purpose) flour

250 ml (9 fl oz/1 cup) milk

60 g (2¼ oz/½ cup) grated low-fat tasty cheese

350 g (12 oz/2¼ cups) macaroni, cooked

1  Melt the butter in a small saucepan. Blend in the flour and cook for 1 minute.

2  Remove the pan from the heat and gradually blend in the milk. Return to the heat and cook, stirring, until the sauce boils and thickens.

3  Reduce the heat and simmer for 3 minutes. Add the grated cheese and stir until melted. Mix the macaroni through the sauce.

**Note:** This creamy, cheesy pasta meal always seems to be a firm favourite with kids. And the dairy it contains is good for young children, being rich in calcium needed for growing teeth and bones.

# pitta pizzas

### SERVES 4

4 large wholemeal (whole-wheat) pitta pocket breads

130 g (4³/₄ oz/¹/₂ cup) tomato salsa

¹/₂ red onion, thinly sliced

90 g (3¹/₄ oz) mushrooms, thinly sliced

60 g (2¹/₄ oz) low-fat ham, thinly sliced

90 g (3¹/₄ oz/¹/₂ cup) black olives in brine, rinsed, drained, pitted and chopped

1 tablespoon capers, rinsed, drained and chopped

80 g (2³/₄ oz/¹/₂ cup) low-fat feta cheese

10 g (¹/₄ oz/¹/₄ cup) sprigs rosemary

100 g (3¹/₂ oz/1 cup) grated reduced-fat mozzarella

1. Preheat the oven to 200°C (400°F/Gas 6). Place the pitta breads on a baking tray.

2. Spread each with the salsa. Top with the onion, mushrooms, ham, olives and capers.

3. Crumble the feta over and top with the rosemary sprigs and mozzarella. Bake for 20 minutes.

**Variations:** Try the following toppings: low-fat ham, pineapple pieces, sliced capsicum (pepper), onion or olives marinated in brine.

For a meaty topping, try leftover savoury minced (ground) beef or spaghetti bolognaise and low-fat cheddar cheese.

For a little spice, try salami, corn kernels, sliced green capsicum, onion, tomato and low-fat feta cheese.

A tasty vegetarian option is artichoke hearts, tomato and zucchini (courgette) slices, ricotta and low-fat feta cheese.

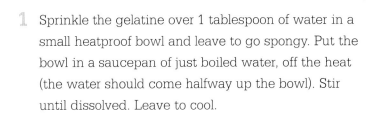

# raspberry mousse

## SERVES 4–6

10 g (¼ oz) powdered gelatine

250 g (9 oz/1 cup) low-fat vanilla yoghurt

400 g (14 oz) light vanilla fromage frais dessert

4 egg whites

150 g (5½ oz/1¼ cups) fresh raspberries, coarsely mashed

fresh raspberries and mint leaves, to serve

1  Sprinkle the gelatine over 1 tablespoon of water in a small heatproof bowl and leave to go spongy. Put the bowl in a saucepan of just boiled water, off the heat (the water should come halfway up the bowl). Stir until dissolved. Leave to cool.

2  Combine the vanilla yoghurt and fromage frais dessert in a large bowl, then add the cooled gelatine and mix.

3  Beat the egg whites until stiff peaks form, then fold through the yoghurt mixture until just combined. Transfer half the mixture to a separate bowl and fold in the mashed raspberries.

4  Divide the raspberry mixture among four tall glasses, then top with the vanilla mixture. Refrigerate for several hours, or until set. Decorate with extra fresh raspberries and mint leaves.

# rice cake snack

## SERVES 1–2

1½ tablespoons unsalted peanut butter

2 rice cakes

1 banana

1 teaspoon honey

1  Spread the peanut butter onto the rice cakes.

2  Slice the banana, and arrange the slices on top of the peanut butter.

3  Drizzle the honey over banana and serve.

**Note:** These are great as a quick after-school snack. They're not suitable for lunchbox snacks because most schools don't allow nut products, due to children having severe nut allergies.

# summer fruity yoghurt

**SERVES 4**

2 ripe pears, unpeeled

2 teaspoon lemon juice

80 g (2³/₄ oz/¹/₂ cup) fresh or frozen blueberries

125 g (4¹/₂ oz) strawberries, hulled, halved and quartered

100 g (3¹/₂ oz) raspberries

pulp of 2 passionfruit

1 tablespoon caster (superfine) sugar

500 g (1 lb 2 oz/2 cups) low-fat vanilla or fruit-flavoured yoghurt

1 Remove the core from the pears. Cut into chunks and put into a large bowl. Sprinkle with the lemon juice.

2 Add the blueberries, strawberries, raspberries and passionfruit and sprinkle with the sugar. Set aside for 10 minutes to infuse.

3 Gently fold in the yoghurt.

4 Spoon into four glasses and chill for at least 20 minutes.

**Hint:** For variety you can also make this recipe with raspberries, nectarines or peaches, or chopped citrus fruits.

# frozen fruit blocks

## MAKES 6

200 ml (7 fl oz) apple juice

2 x 140 g (5 oz) tinned fruit in natural juice

1 tablespoon fresh passionfruit pulp

1 Combine the fruits, juice and pulp in a small bowl.

2 Spoon the mixture carefully into six plastic ice-block moulds with sticks.

3 Put in the freezer and allow to set overnight. When frozen, unmould ice-blocks and serve.

**Notes:** Ice-block moulds are available in the supermarket and selected kitchenware shops.

Use any canned fruits, pears, peaches, apricots, pineapple, fruit salad or two fruits. If fruit pieces are large, they may need to be chopped more finely.

# berry jellies

**SERVES 4**

85 g (3 oz) sachet raspberry-flavoured jelly crystals

250 g (9 oz) mixed frozen or fresh berries (defrosted if using frozen)

2 tablespoons sugar

200 g (7 oz) low-fat vanilla yoghurt

1  Put the jelly crystals in a bowl and pour over 250 ml (9 fl oz/1 cup) of boiling water. Stir to dissolve the crystals then add 250 ml (9 fl oz/ 1 cup) of cold water.

2  Spoon 2 tablespoons of the jelly into each of four 200 ml (7 fl oz) parfait glasses. Refrigerate until set.

3  When the berries have defrosted, strain and add any berry juices to the remaining jelly. Gently stir the sugar into the berries.

4  Divide most of the fruit over the set jelly in the parfait glasses. Pour the remaining jelly over the fruit. Refrigerate for 2 hours, or until firm.

5  Carefully spoon the yoghurt over the jellies and smooth the surface. Garnish with the leftover berries.

**Note:** If using fresh berries, try 3–4 different varieties such as small hulled strawberries, blueberries, raspberries and blackberries.

# pear slushy

### SERVES 4–6

800 g (1 lb 12 oz) tinned pear halves in syrup

1 teaspoon citric acid

1. Put the pears, their syrup and the citric acid into a blender. Blend on high for 2–3 minutes.

2. Pour into a shallow metal tin and freeze for about 1 hour, or until just frozen around the edges.

3. Scrape the ice back into the mixture with a fork. Repeat every 30 minutes until the mixture consists of even-sized ice crystals.

4. Serve immediately. Allow to soften slightly in the refrigerator before serving.

5. Pile into long cups and serve with a spoon and a straw.

# watermelon slushy

### SERVES 6

2 kg (4 lb 8 oz/10 cups) chopped watermelon (about 1 large watermelon)

250 g (9 oz) strawberries, hulled

2 teaspoons caster (superfine) sugar

1. Combine the watermelon, strawberries and sugar in bowl. Put the mixture in a food processor and blend until smooth.

2. Pour into a shallow metal tray. Cover with plastic wrap and freeze for 2–3 hours, or until the mixture begins to freeze.

3. Return to the blender and blend quickly to break up the ice.

4. Pour into 6 glasses, then cut the reserved watermelon into 6 small triangles and fix one onto the edge of each glass.

# razzle dazzle

### SERVES 2

1 lime

150g (5½ oz) raspberries

1 teaspoon natural vanilla extract

200g (7 oz) strawberry frozen yoghurt

1. Juice the lime in a citrus press.

2. Blend the raspberries, lime juice, vanilla and frozen yoghurt in a blender or food processor until smooth.

# strawberry shake

### SERVES 2

1 small, ripe banana, chopped

90 g (3¼ oz/½ cup) chopped strawberries

250 ml (9 fl oz/1 cup) milk

3 scoops ice cream

1. Put the banana, strawberries, milk and ice cream in a blender or food processor.

2. Blend on high speed for 1 minute or until the mixture is smooth.

## yoghurt shake

**SERVES 1**

250 ml (9 fl oz/1 cup) low-fat milk

125 g (4½ oz/½ cup) frozen yoghurt

½ banana

1   Put all ingredients in a blender and blend 1 minute. Pour into glass to serve.

## choc-mint dream

**SERVES 2**

4 scoops choc-mint ice cream

375 g (13 fl oz) milk

chocolate sprinkles

1   Put 2 scoops of ice cream and milk in blender. Blend until smooth.

2   Pour into a glass. Top each with a scoop of ice cream and chocolate sprinkles.

## vanilla milkshake

**SERVES 2**

500 ml (17 fl oz/ 2 cups) milk, well chilled

1 teaspoon natural vanilla extract

sugar, to taste

1   Put the milk, vanilla extract and sugar into a large bowl or blender and whisk or blend for 20 seconds to combine.

2   Pour into two long cups and serve with straws for fun.

**Note:** There is nothing wrong with adding flavouring to milk to encourage enjoyment. Research has shown that children who drink milk are often taller and have healthier bones and body weights than those who don't.

## carob milkshake

**SERVES 2**

1 tablespoon carob powder

1 tablespoon sugar

500 ml (17 fl oz/2 cups) milk, well chilled

40 g (1½ oz/¼ cup) finely chopped carob buttons

1   Dissolve the carob powder and sugar in 1 tablespoon hot water. Allow to cool.

1   Whisk the milk and carob mixture together. Pour into long glasses. Top with the carob.

**Hint:** This milkshake is rich in calcium and phosphorus, excellent for strong bones and teeth.

# index

Published in 2008 by Murdoch Books Pty Limited

Murdoch Books Australia
Pier 8/9
23 Hickson Road
Millers Point NSW 2000
Phone: +61 (0) 2 8220 2000
Fax: +61 (0) 2 8220 2558
www.murdochbooks.com.au

Murdoch Books UK Limited
Erico House
6th Floor
93–99 Upper Richmond Road
Putney, London SW15 2TG
Phone: +44 (0) 20 8785 5995
Fax: +44 (0) 20 8785 5985
www.murdochbooks.co.uk

Chief Executive: Juliet Rogers
Publishing Director: Kay Scarlett

Design Manager: Vivien Valk
Design concept, art direction and design: Alex Frampton
Project Manager and Editor: Gordana Trifunovic
Production: Kita George
Photographer: Michele Aboud
Stylist: Sarah DeNardi
Food preparation: Julie Ray and Simon Ruffell

National Library of Australia Cataloguing-in-Publication Data
Broadhurst, Lucy. Ready, steady, lunchbox. Includes index.
ISBN 978 1 74196 274 1 (pbk.)
1. Lunchbox cookery. 2. Cookery—Juvenile literature. I. Title. 641.534

Printed by i-Book Printing Ltd. in 2008. PRINTED IN CHINA.
The publisher and stylist would like to thank Spotlight, Kek, Kitsch Kitchen, Rice, Knox and Floyd and Echidna Place for lending props and equipment for photography.
Many thanks to our models Mia, Isolde, Ruby, Ava, Felix and Nell.

IMPORTANT: Those who might be at risk from the effects of salmonella poisoning (the elderly, pregnant women, young children and those suffering from immune deficiency diseases) should consult their doctor with any concerns about eating raw eggs.

CONVERSION GUIDE: You may find cooking times vary depending on the oven you are using. For fan-forced ovens, as a general rule, set the oven temperature to 20°C (35°F) lower than indicated in the recipe. We have used 20 ml (4 teaspoon) tablespoon measures. If you are using a 15 ml (3 teaspoon) tablespoon, for most recipes the difference will not be noticeable. However, for recipes using baking powder, gelatine, bicarbonate of soda (baking soda), small amounts of flour and cornflour (cornstarch), add an extra teaspoon for each tablespoon specified.